PROGRESSIVE

HEAVY METAL BASS LICKS

VOLUME 1

BY STEPHAN RICHTER

60 MINUTE STEREO CASSETTE AVAILABLE

All the examples in Progressive Heavy Metal Bass Guitar Licks, Volume 1, have been recorded on to a 60 minute STEREO cassette tape.

Acknowledgements

Cover: Phil Martin
Rock Photographs: Neil Zlozower
Instruments supplied by Derringers Music

Distributed by

in **Australia**
Koala Publications Pty. Ltd.
4 Captain Cook Ave.
Flinders Park 5025
South Australia
Ph (08) 268 1750
Fax 61-8-352-4760

in **U.S.A.**
Koala Publications Inc.
3001 Redhill Ave.
Bldg. 2 # 104
Costa Mesa CA
U.S.A. 92626
Ph (714) 546 2743
Fax 1-714-546-2749

in **U.K. and Europe**
Music Exchange
Claverton Rd.
Wythenshawe
Manchester
M23 9NE
England
Ph (061) 946 1234
Fax (061) 946 1195

ISBN 0 947183 61 2

Introduction

Progressive Heavy Metal Bass Guitar Licks Volume 1 and *Volume 2* contain Licks that incorporate all the important techniques used by the world's best heavy metal bass players. (These techniques are outlined in *Progressive Heavy Metal Method for Bass Guitar* and *Heavy Metal Techniques for Bass Guitar*).

The Licks in these books are particularly useful as reinforcements of:

1) Technical aspects of playing heavy metal bass.
2) A source of ideas for your own licks and solos.
3) Practical exercises.
4) A source of teaching material.

Many of the licks are from well known solos or adaptations of these solos. It is important that after a while you begin to play these licks with some variations of your own. Combine the study of these licks with constant playing and listening. All metal bass players use the same basics but development of style is determined by how these basics are used.

Both music and TAB notation are used. For music readers most of the licks in the two volumes have accidentals (sharps, flats) placed in front of the note to be played. In some cases a key signature is used. For more information on key signatures, reading music and TAB notation see *Progressive Bass Guitar*.

Chord symbols are used to give an indication of what a guitarist would play and how the bass line relates to chords.

The technique to use is mentioned before and/or above each lick e.g. use of hammer-on, pick etc. If nothing is specified use your right hand fingers to play the lick. To make reading easier and to find the notes faster on the fretboard, tablature notation is used. Also fingering numbers are used to help you find the easiest way of playing a lick.

Due to the speed, phrasing and range of heavy metal bass licks they are quite often very hard to read from written music. For this reason it is essential to have the cassette tape that contains all the examples in this book. The book tells you where to locate your fingers and what technique to use and the tape lets you hear how the lick should sound.

Volume 1 and Volume 2 both contain licks from beginner to professional level.

Good luck and have fun.

Stephan Richter

Stephan Richter obtained his degree in Classical Music (Cello major) at the Zurich Conservatorium of Music in Switzerland. He further studied in New York on Electric Bass with Rick Laird and Tony Oppenheim. He currently works as a session musician and teacher. Stephan is author of Progressive Slap Technique for Bass, Tapping Technique for Bass, Heavy Metal Method and Heavy Metal Techniques for Bass, and Heavy Metal Licks Volume 1 and 2.

Symbols and Abbreviations

The Left Hand

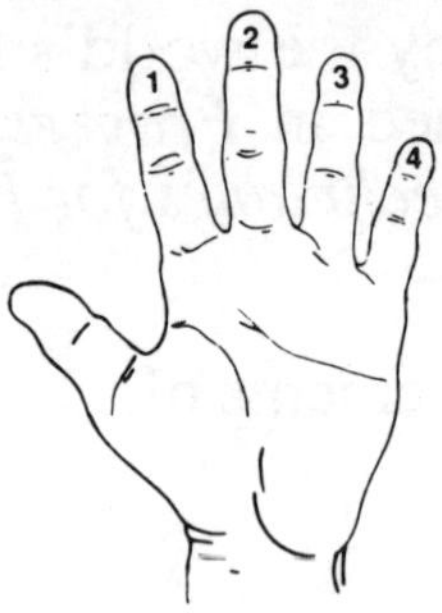

1 = Index finger
2 = Middle finger
3 = Ring finger
4 = Little finger

The Right Hand

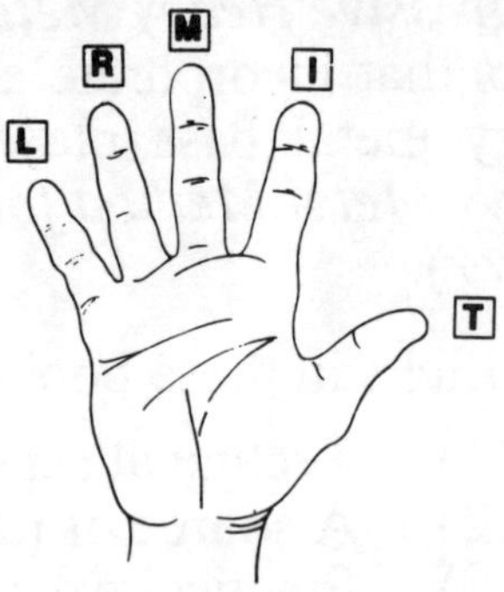

T = Thumb finger
I = Index finger
M = Middle finger
R = Ring finger
L = Little finger

staccato (short detached note)

Hammer-on; generate the sound of a note with the force of your "fretting" finger. Do not "pick" the note.

Quick Hammer-on

Slide - into the indicated note

Slide - only the first note is picked

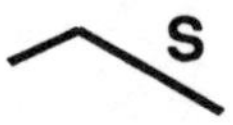

Slide - commence the slide somewhere further up the neck

Slide - quick

PO Pull-off

Symbols and Abbreviations (cont.)

~~	Vibrato
×	Ghost Notes - mute
D (arc)	Dampen
V	Up-pick motion or strum
Λ	Down-pick or strum
↑ (wavy)	Up-strum or raking
↓ (wavy)	Down-strum or raking
(harmonic note)	Harmonic
T	Thumb slap or tap with the thumb
P	Popping Effect
▽	Wood Slapping
HA	Hammer Attack
↓	Tapping right hand
I ↓	Tapping using Index finger
I M ↓	Tapping Index and Middle finger together

Gene Simmons (Kiss)

Don Dokken

Tablature

Tablature is a method of indicating the position of notes on the fretboard. There are four "tab" lines, each representing one of the four strings on the bass.

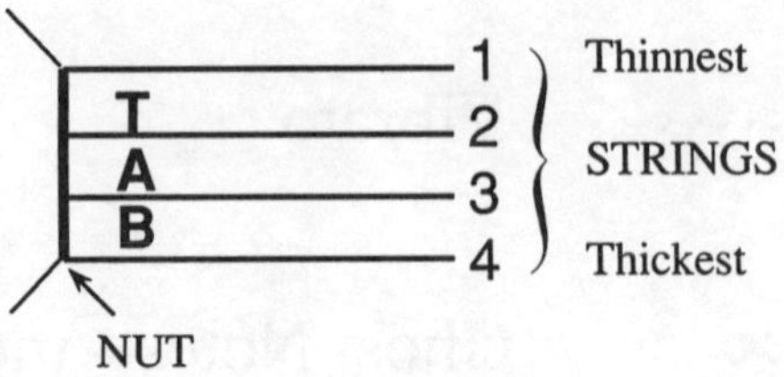

When a number is placed on one of the lines, it indicates the fret location of a note, e.g.

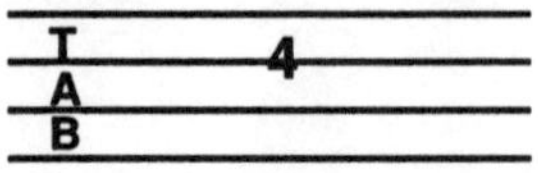

This indicates the 4th fret of the second string (an F♯ note).

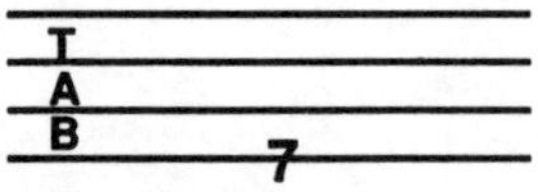

This indicates the 7th fret of the 4th string (a B note).

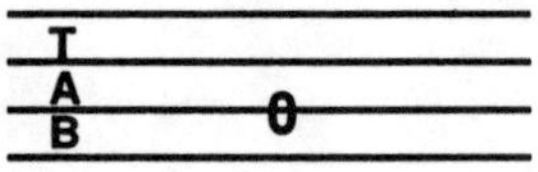

This indicates the third string open (an A note).

Rudy Sarzo (Whitesnake)

1

2

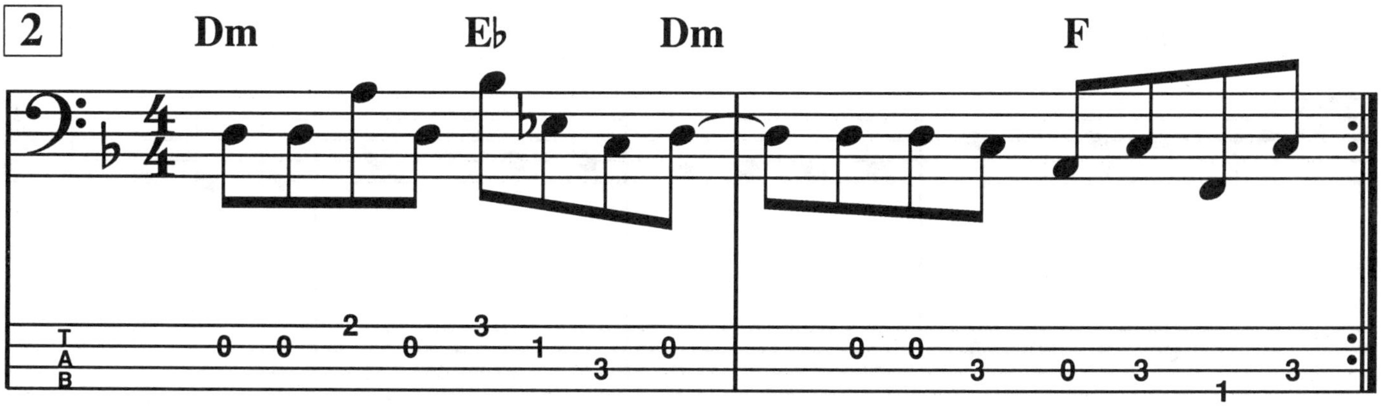

3

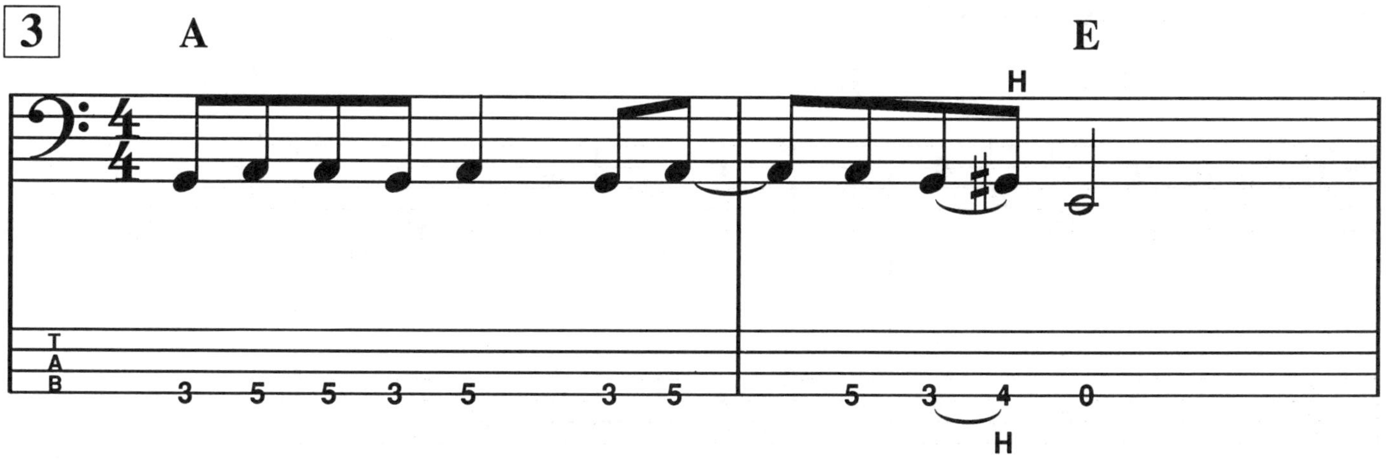

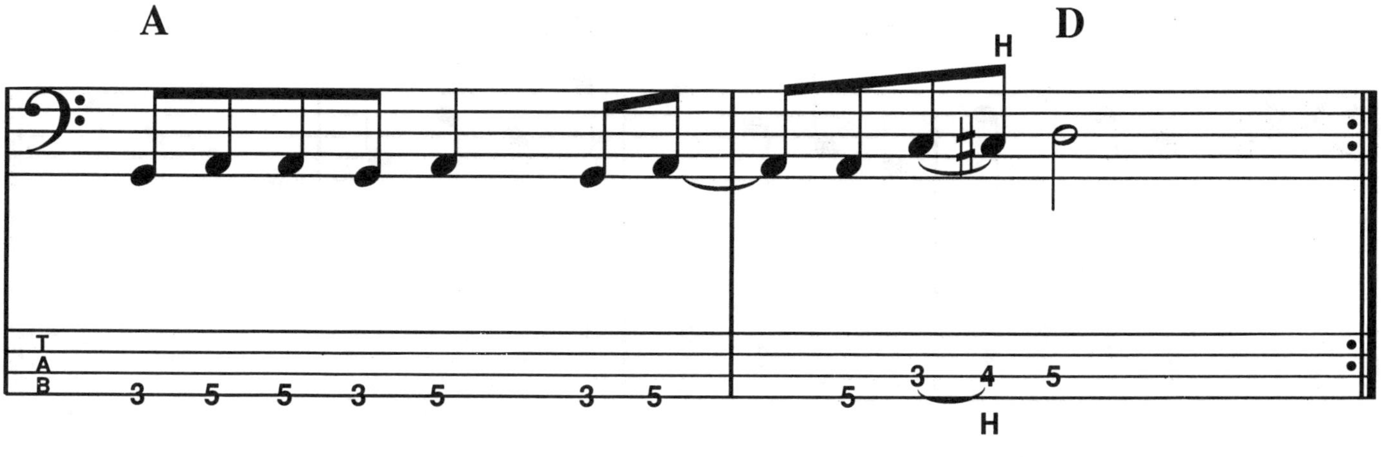

Licks 4-6 use the same chord progression.

4

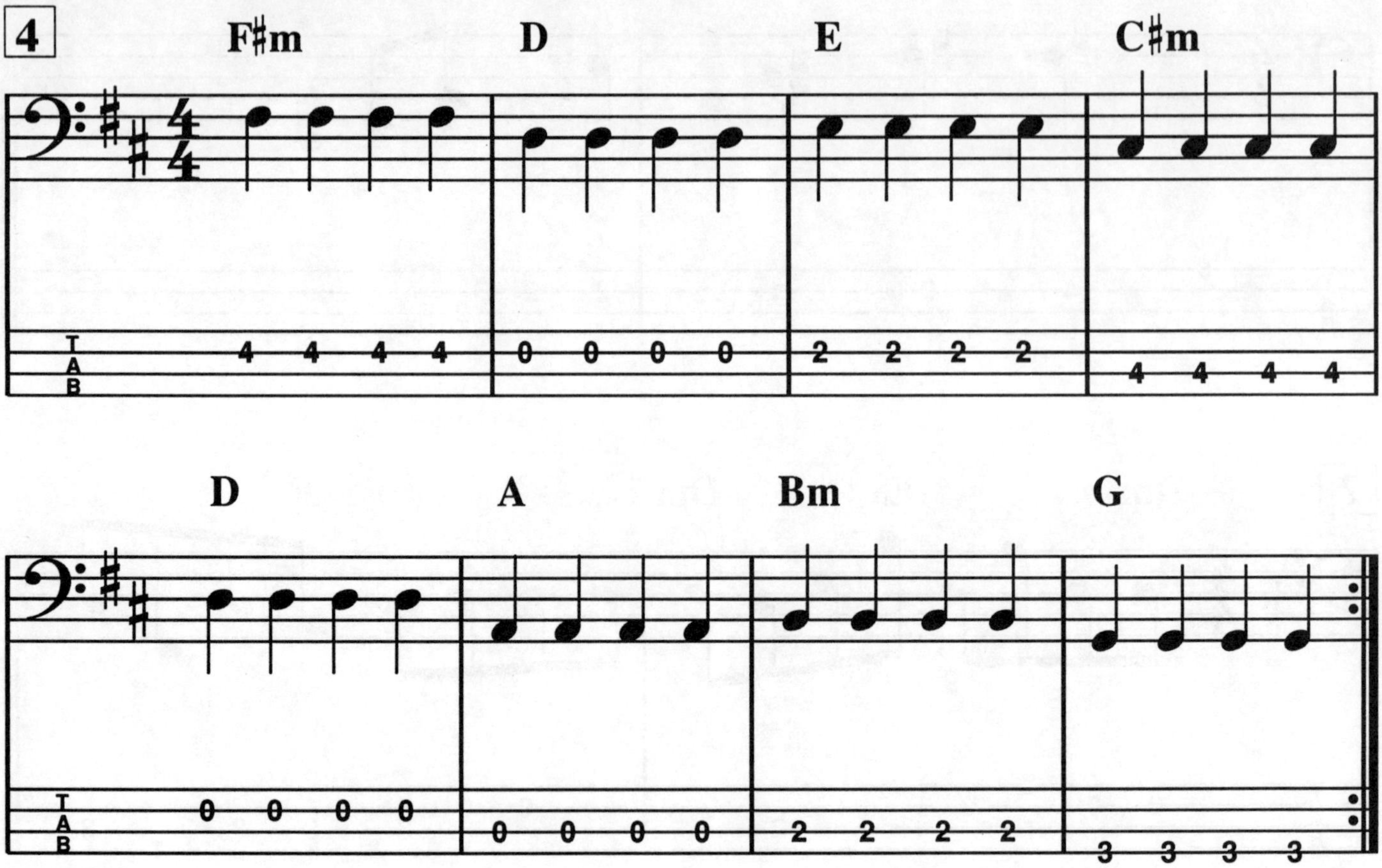

Lick 5 uses chord notes only.

5

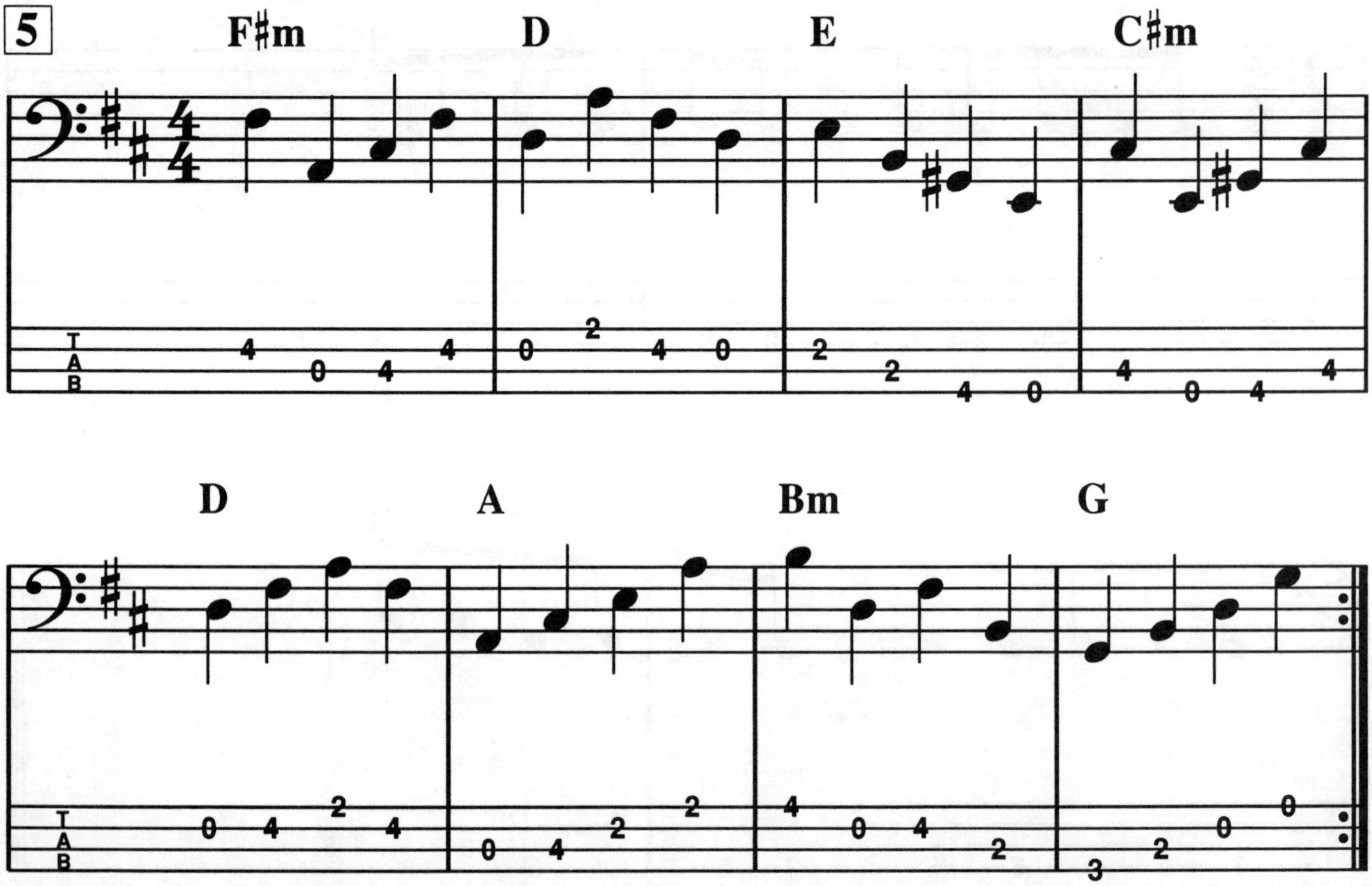

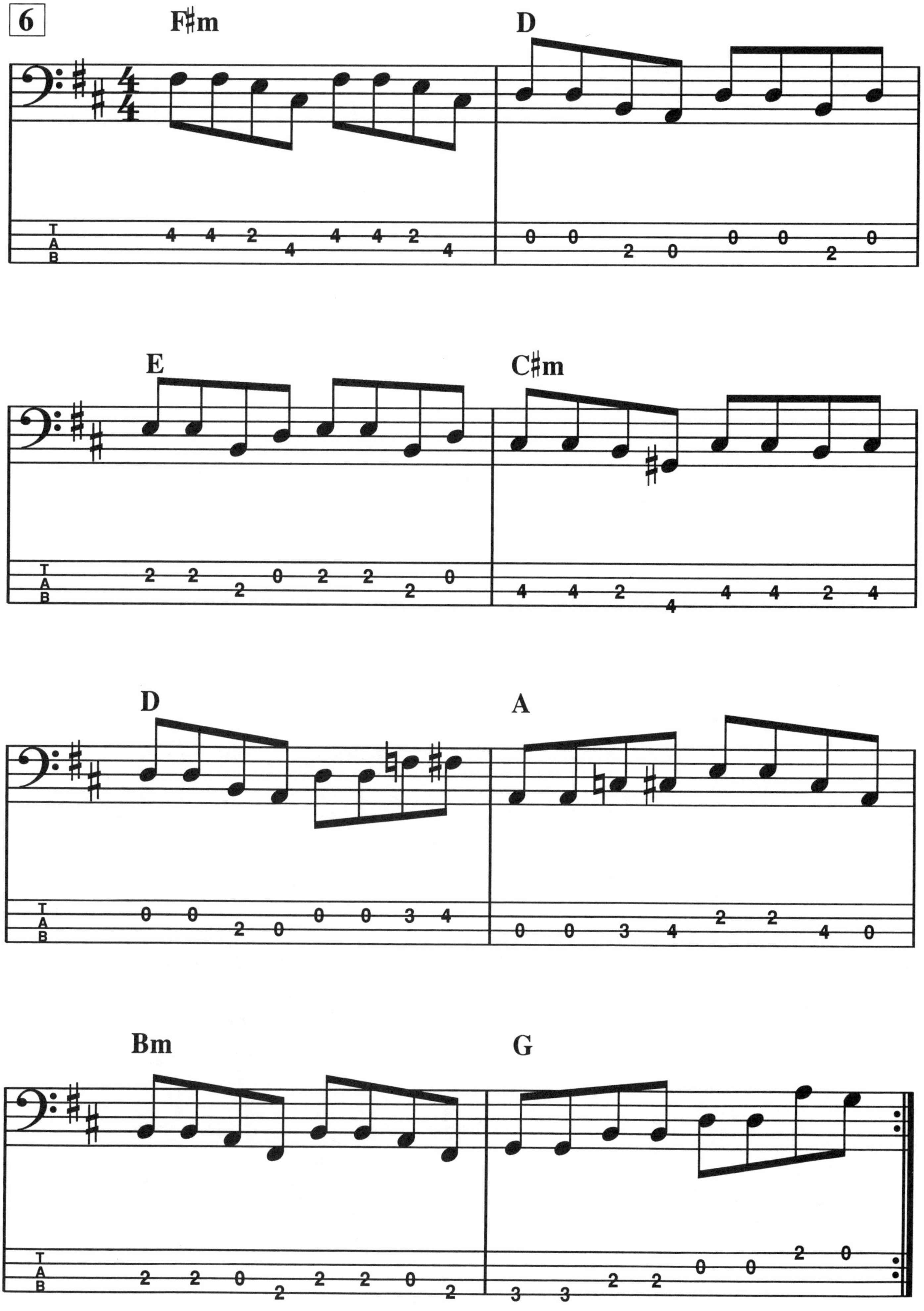
6
F♯m
D
E
C♯m
D
A
Bm
G
T
A
B

7

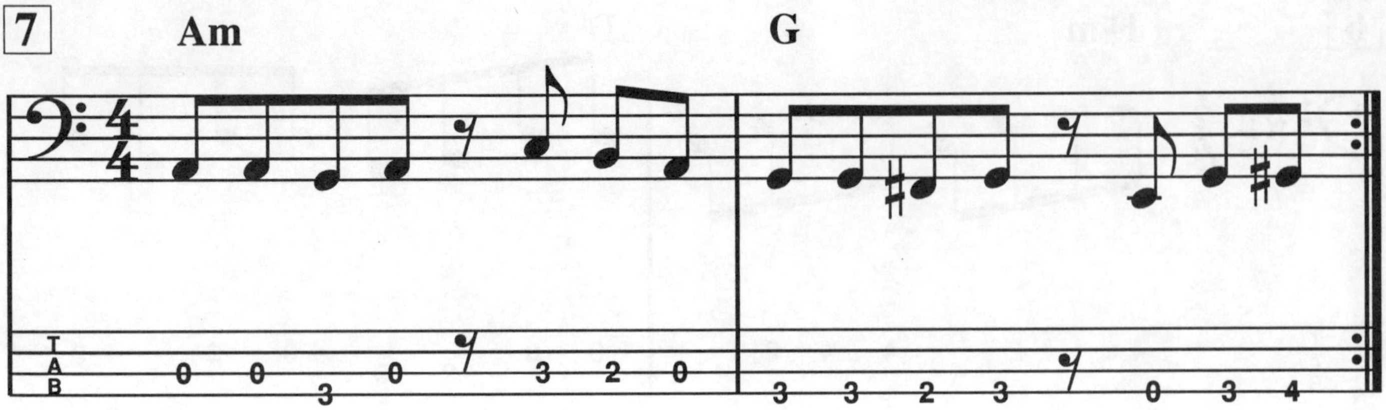

8

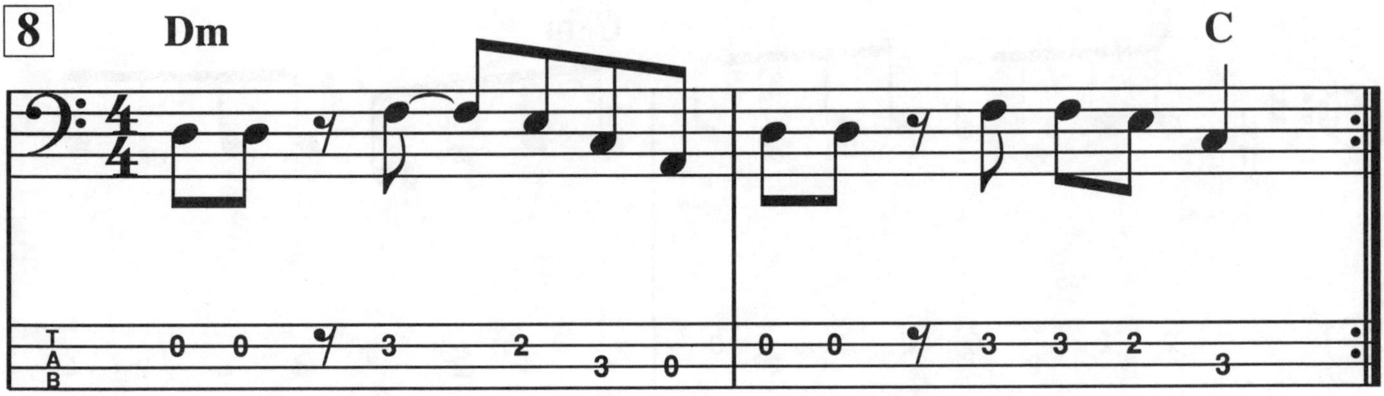

AC/DC

9

10

11

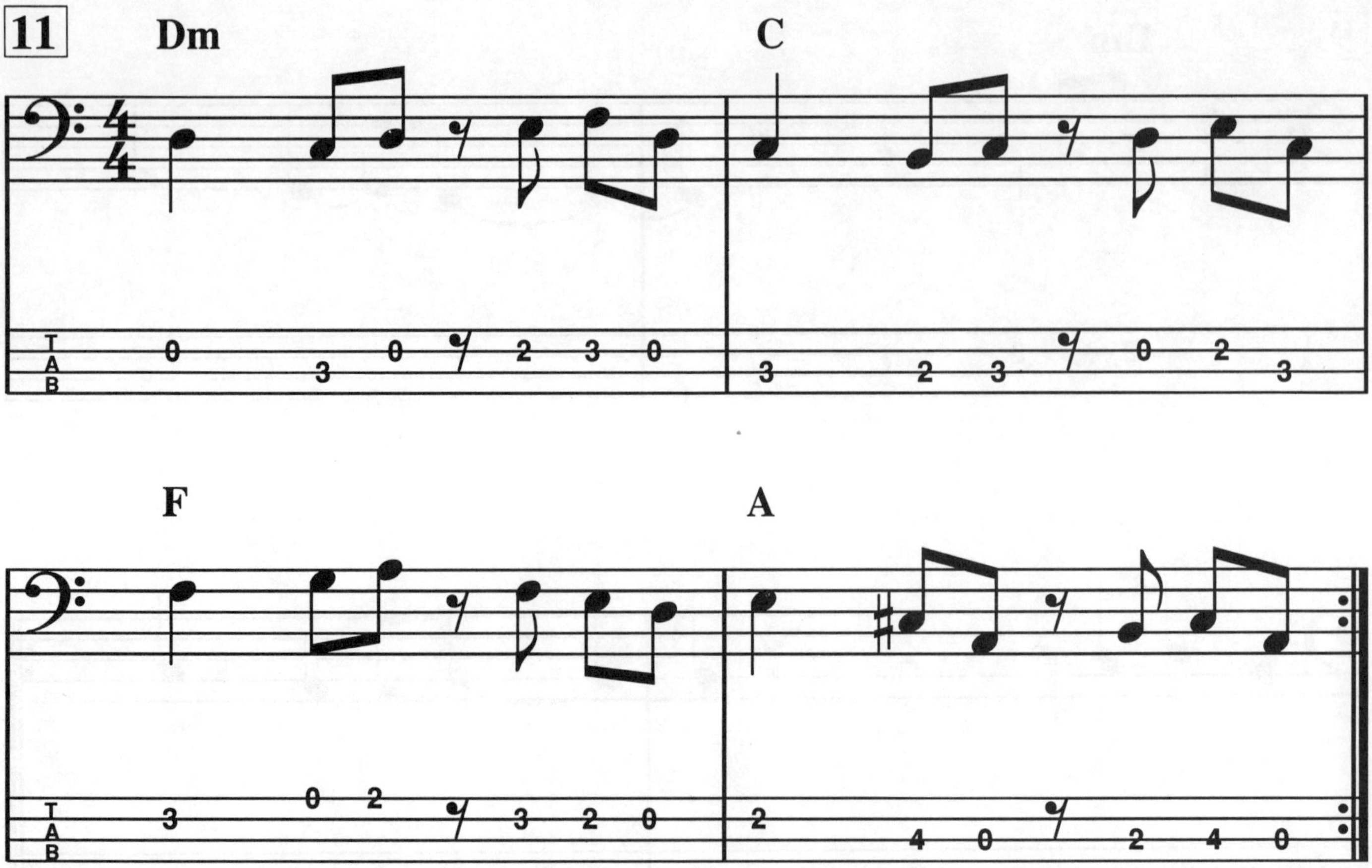

Play the first two bars of this lick four times (*4x*) before playing the last two bars.

12

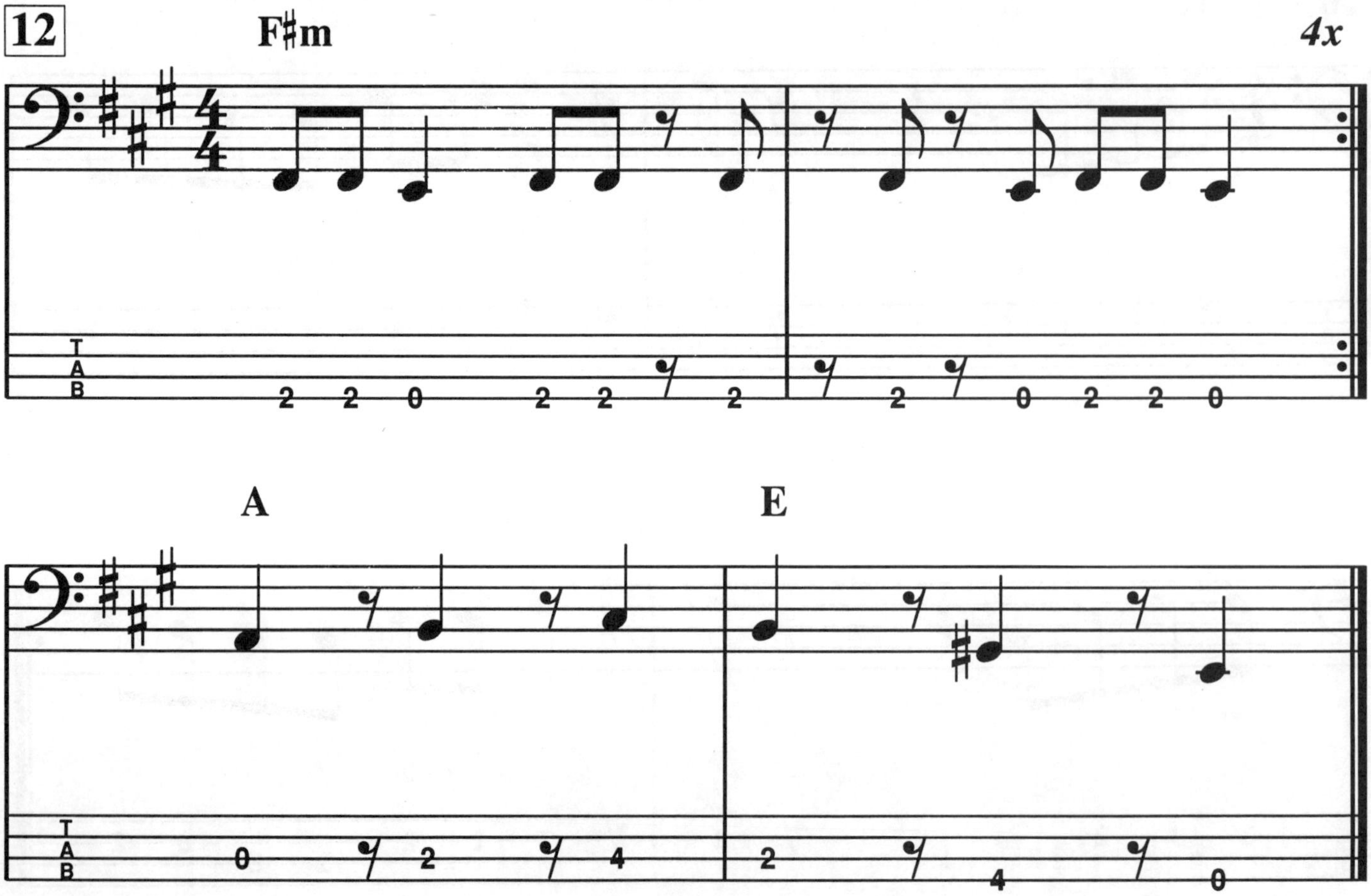

13

14

15

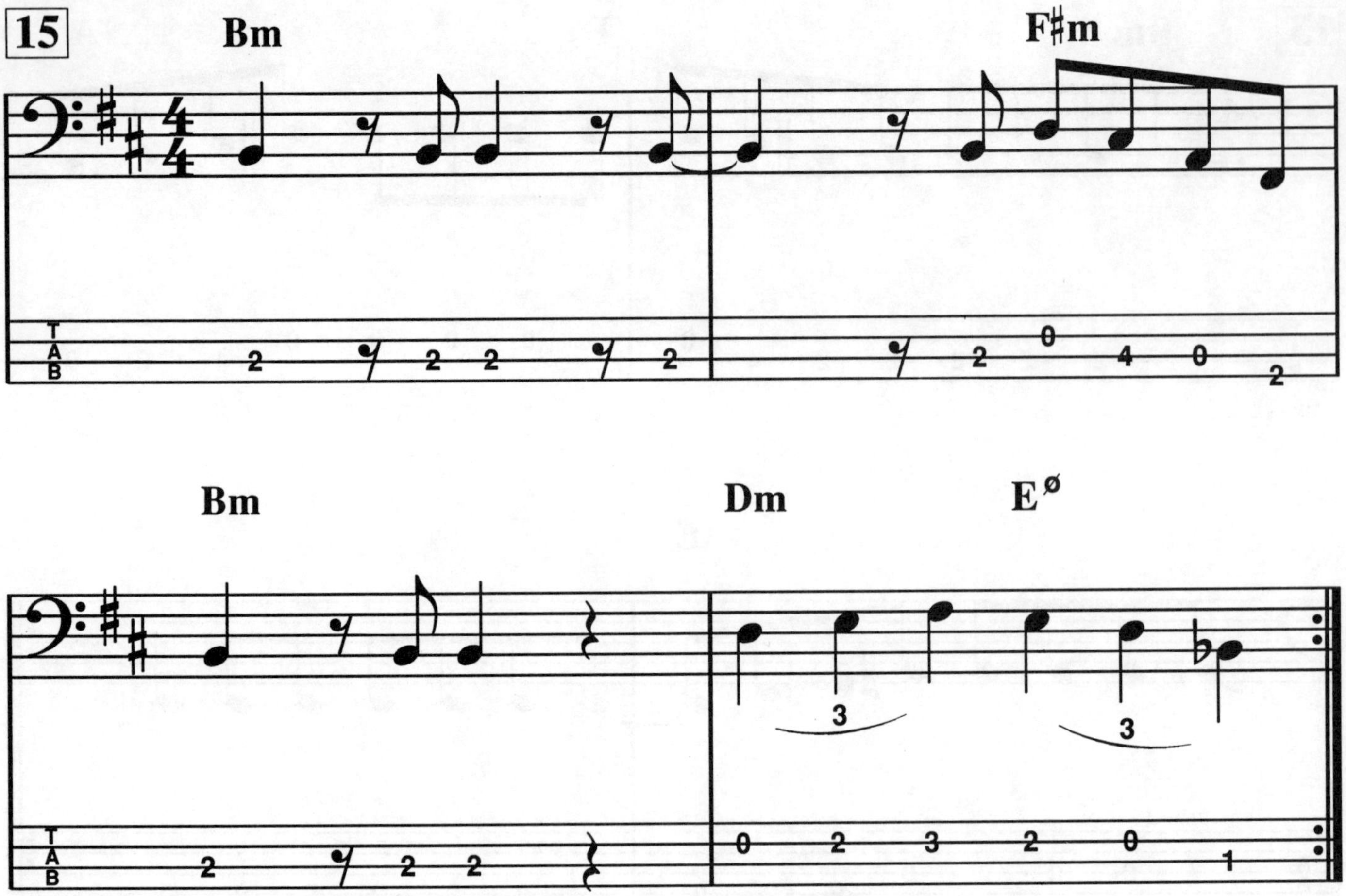

16

17

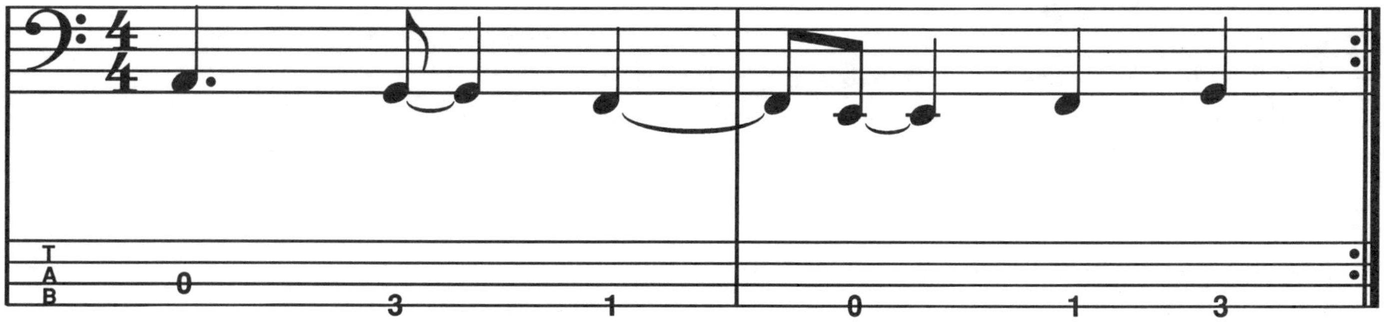

18

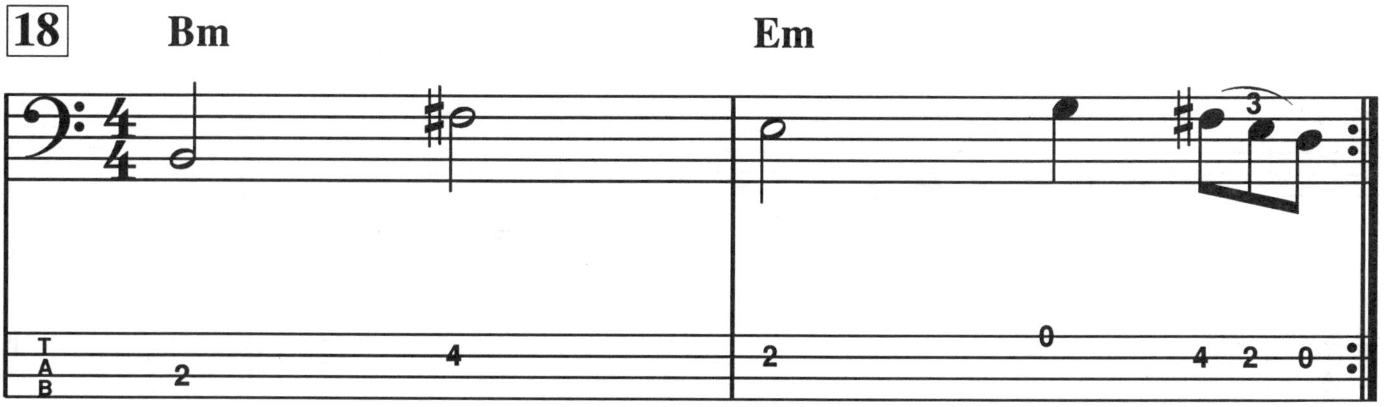

Metallica

19

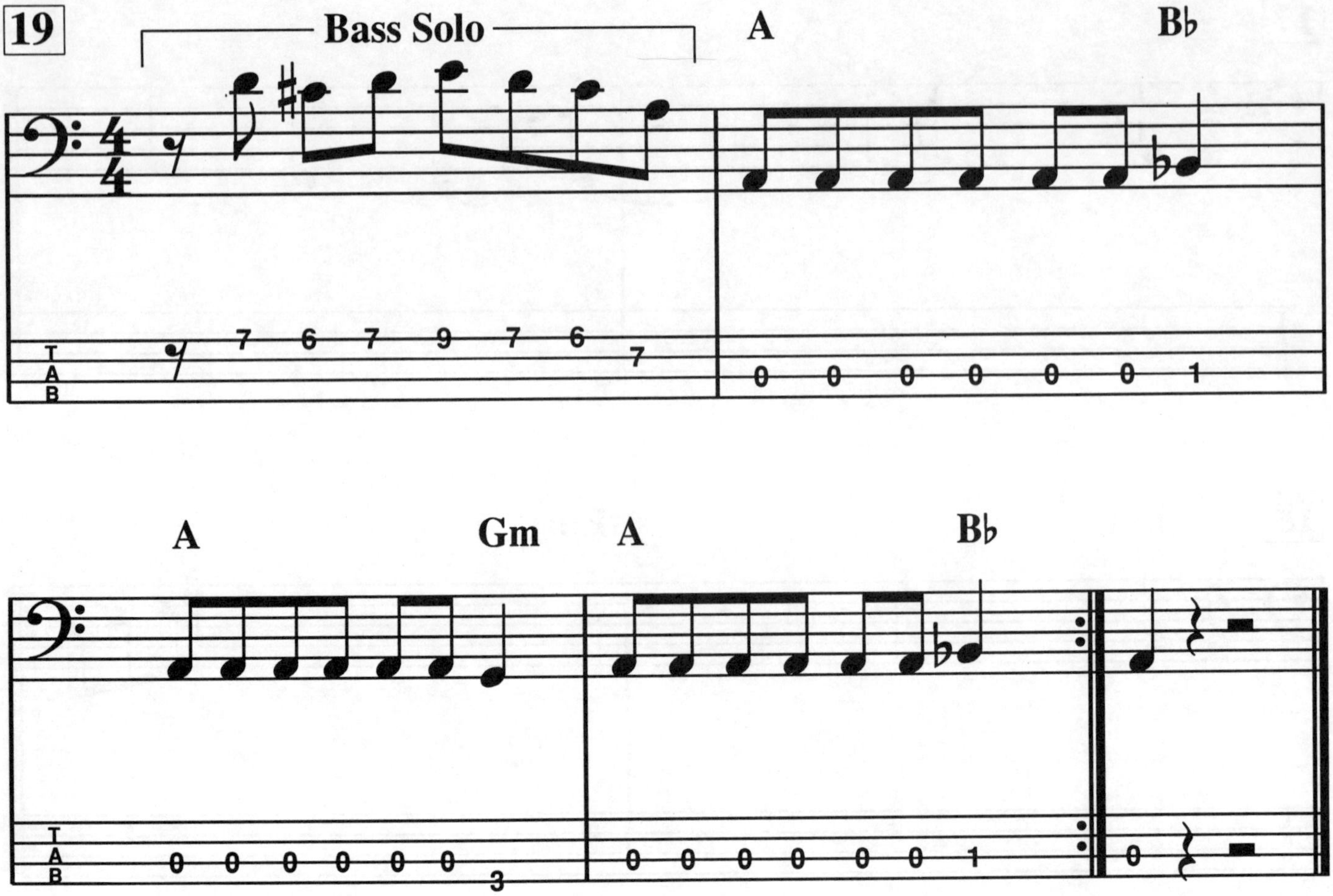
Bass Solo
A
B♭
T
A
B
7 6 7 9 7 6 7
0 0 0 0 0 0 1
A
Gm
A
B♭
0 0 0 0 0 0 3
0 0 0 0 0 0 1
0

20

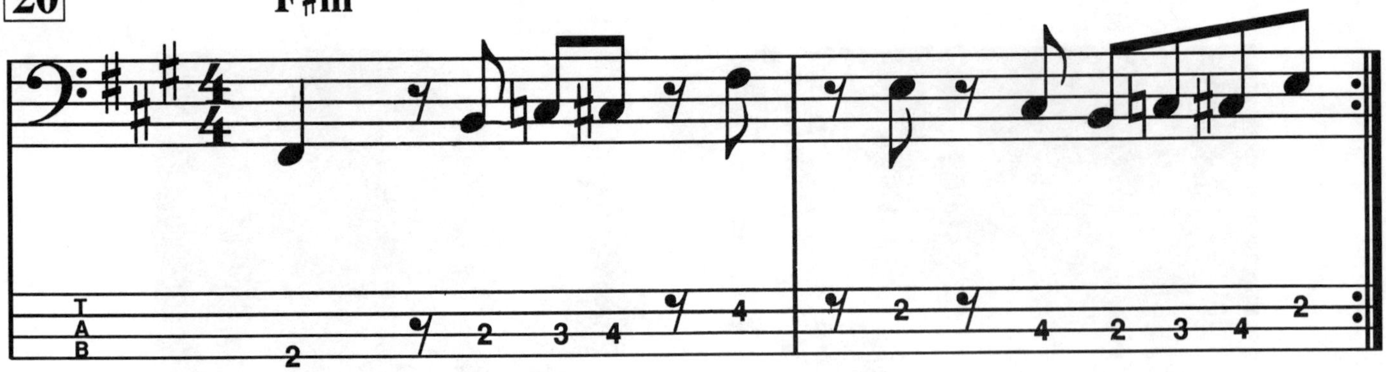
F♯m
T
A
B
2 2 3 4 4
2 4 2 3 4 2

21

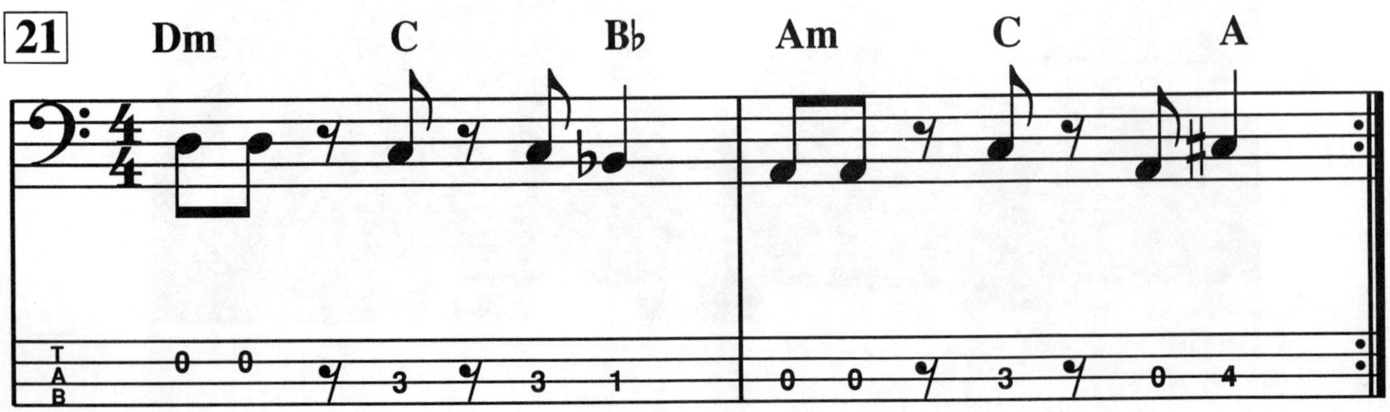
Dm
C
B♭
Am
C
A
T
A
B
0 0 3 3 1
0 0 3 0 4

Lick 22 can be played with the slapping technique, the pick or fingers.

22

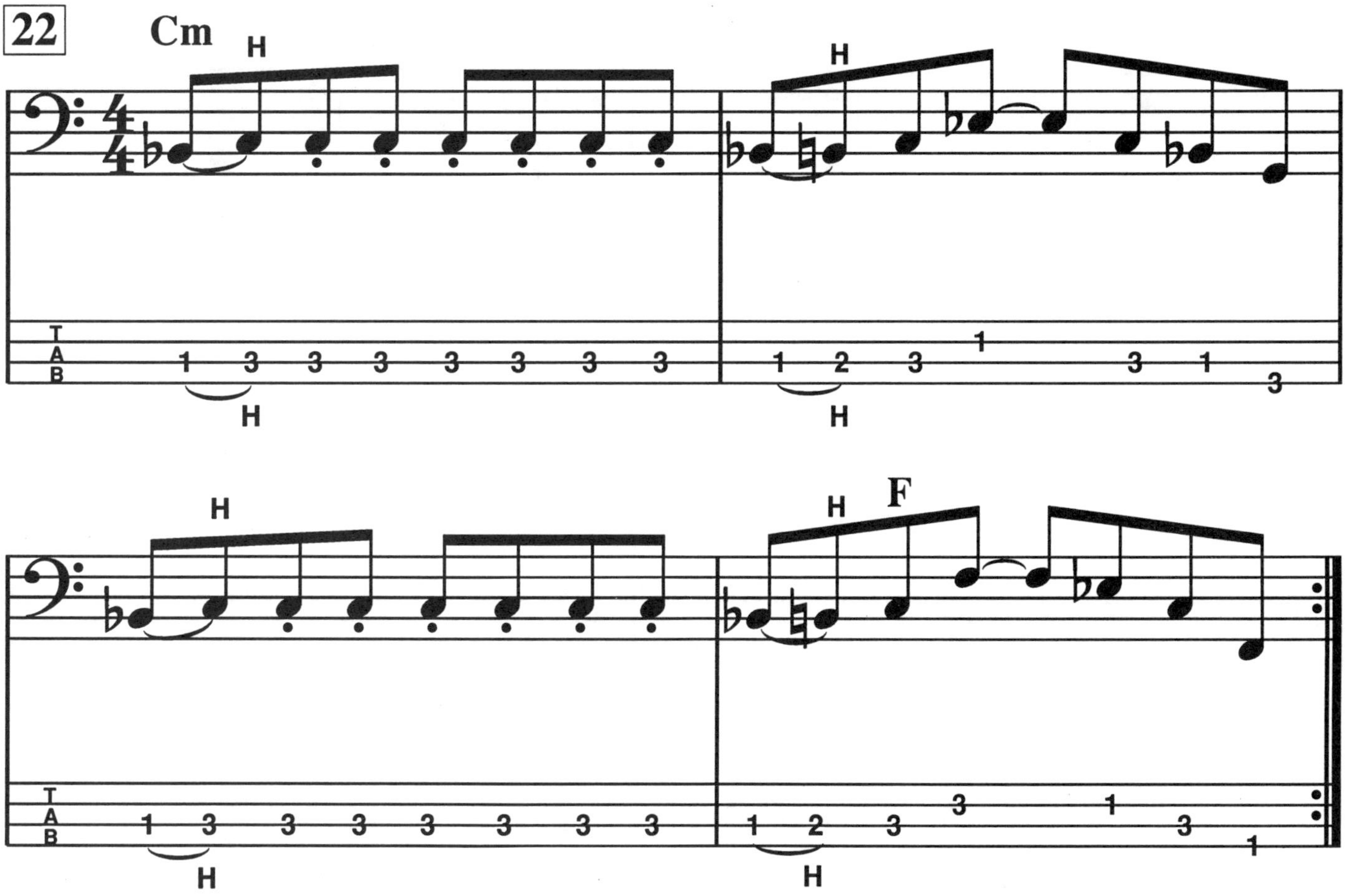

23

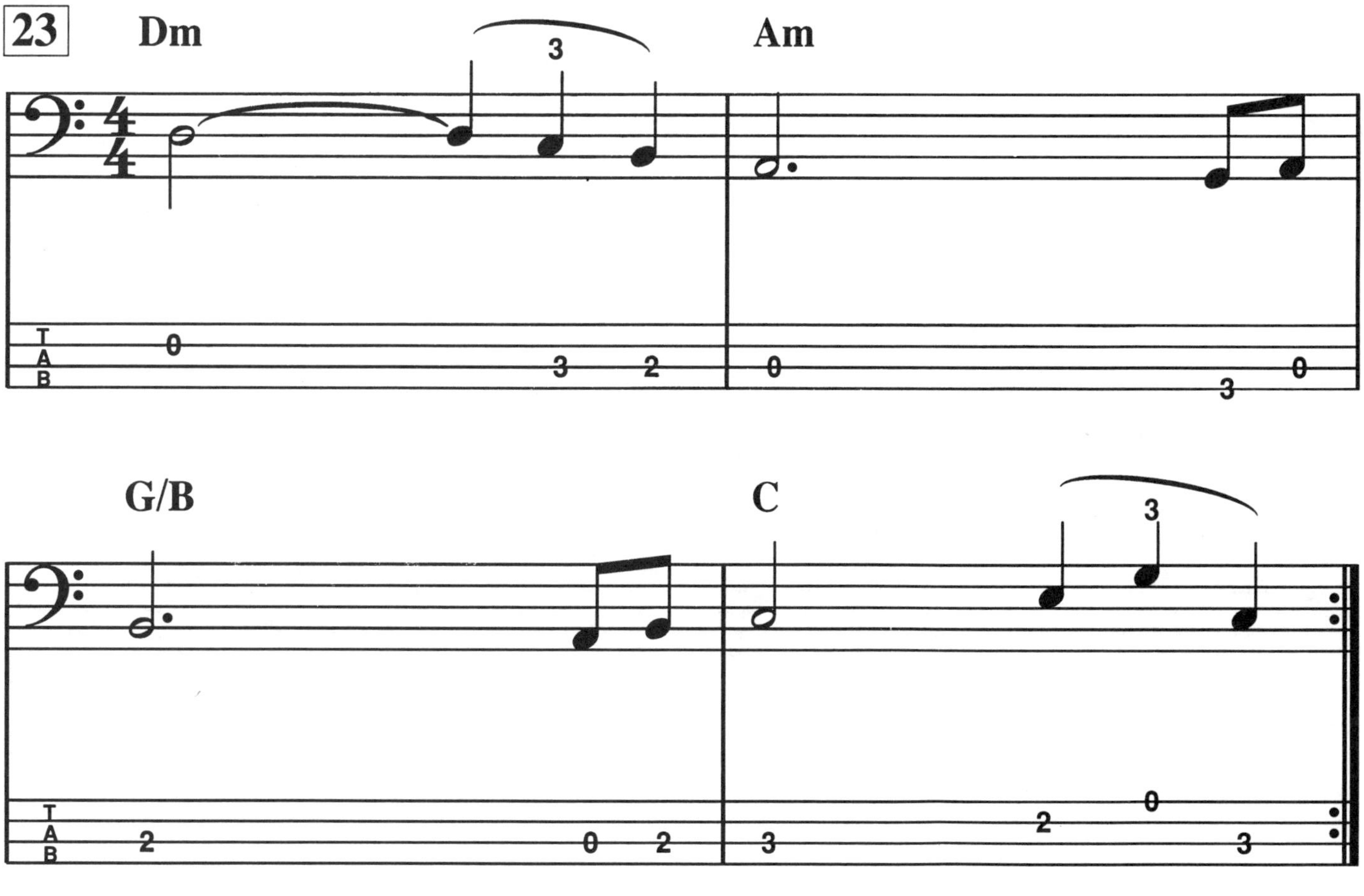

Use a pick for this lick.

24

First and Second Bar Ending

Lick 25 introduces **First and Second Endings**. On the first time through the progression, ending one is played (1.), then the progression is repeated (as indicated by the repeat sign), and ending two is played (2.). Be careful not to play both endings together.

25

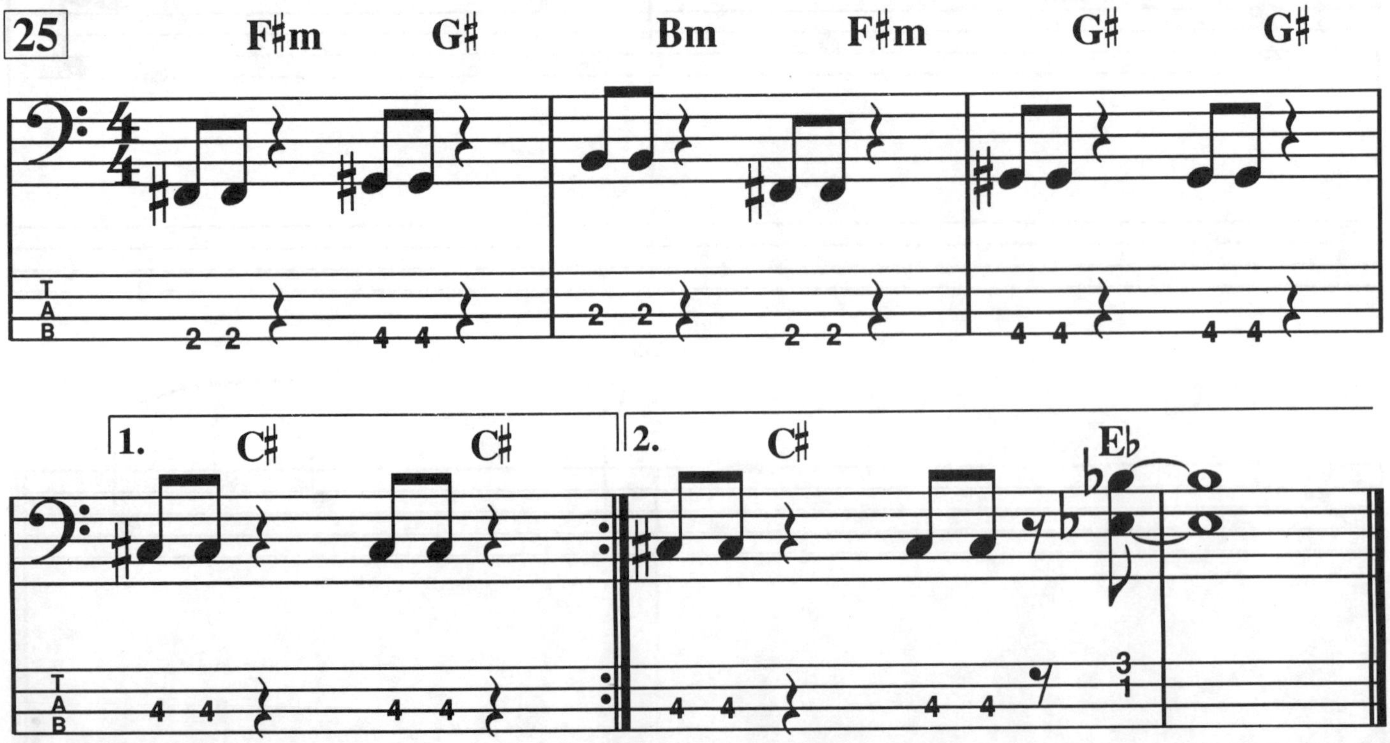

Use the fingers, pick or slapping technique to play this lick.

26

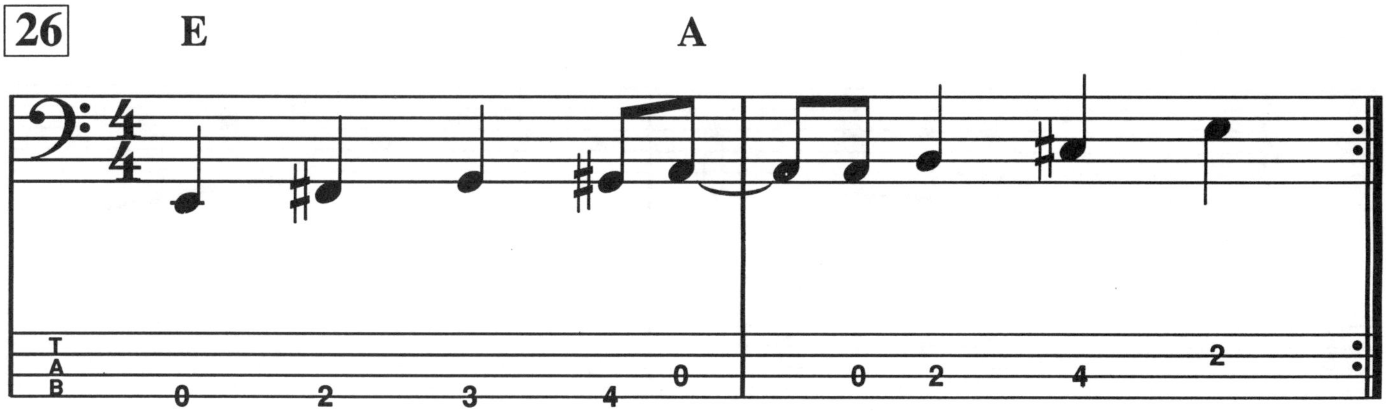

27

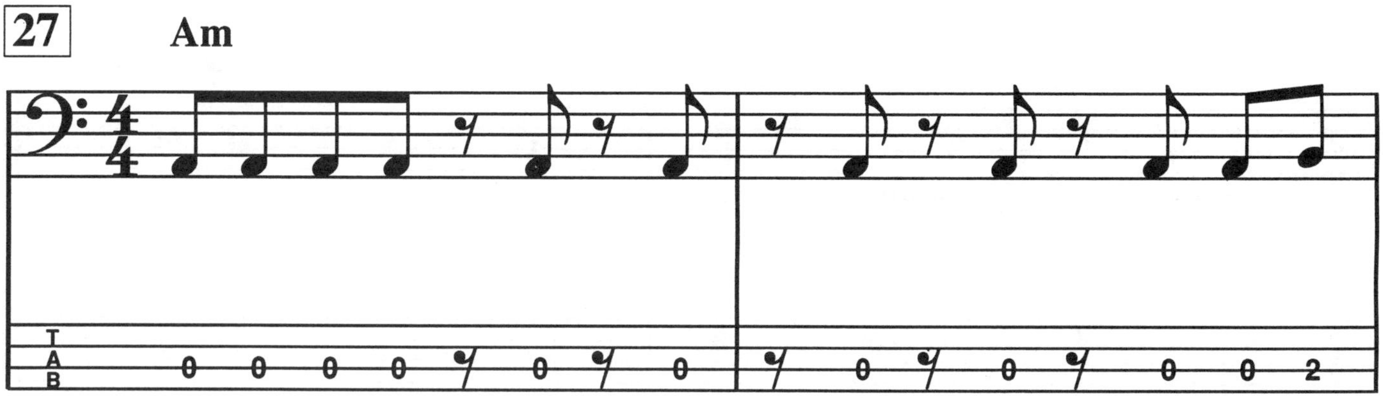

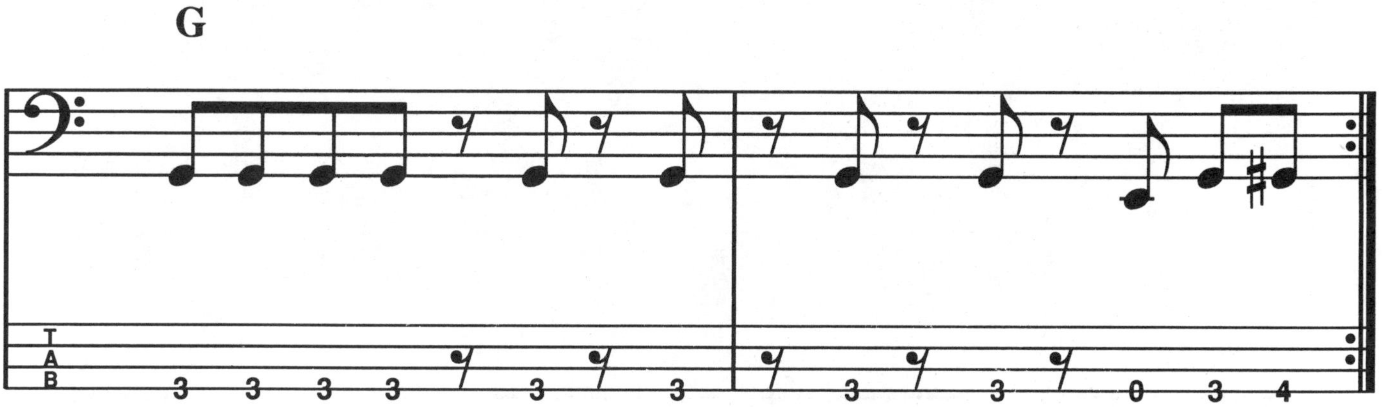

28

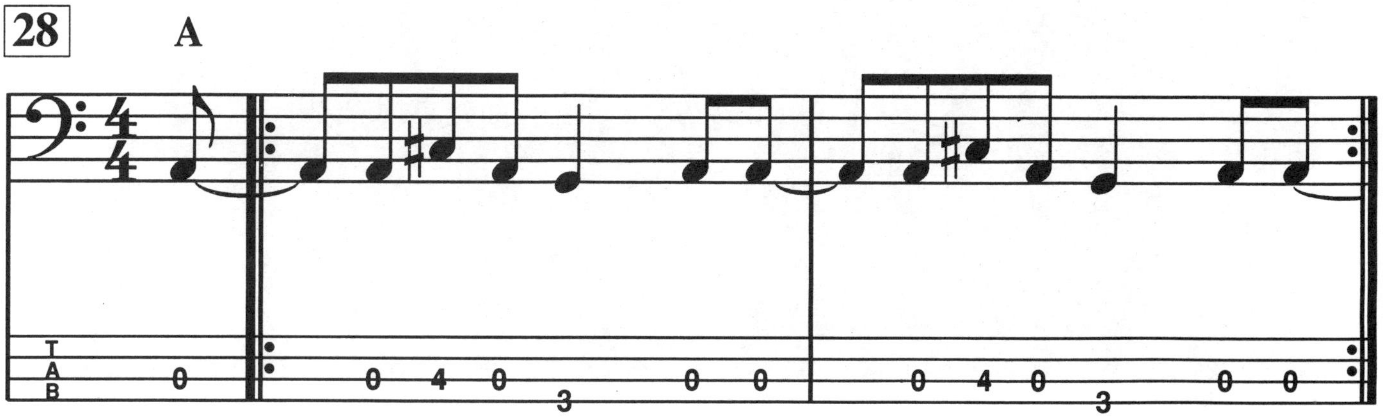

29

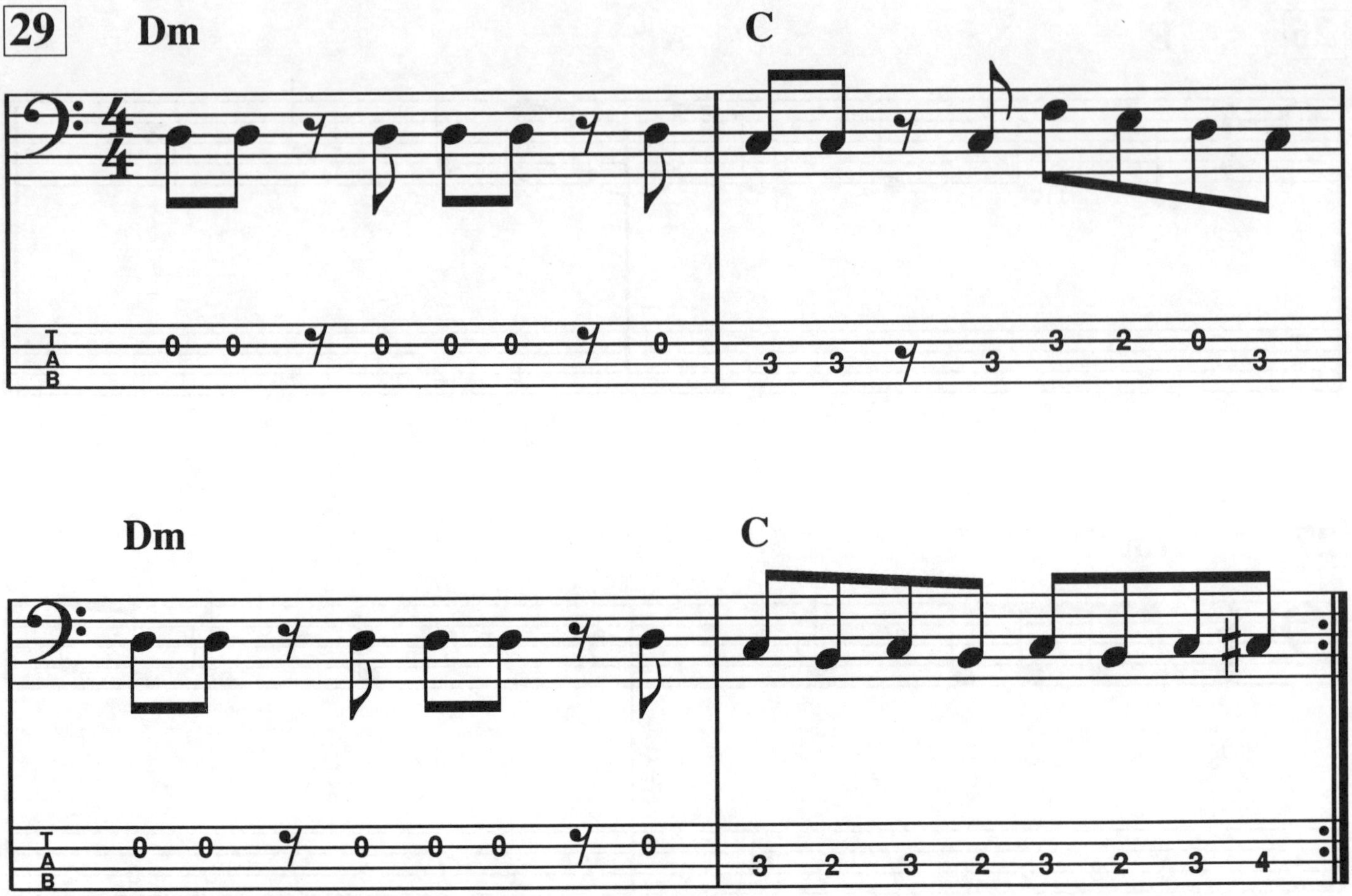

Iron Maiden

30

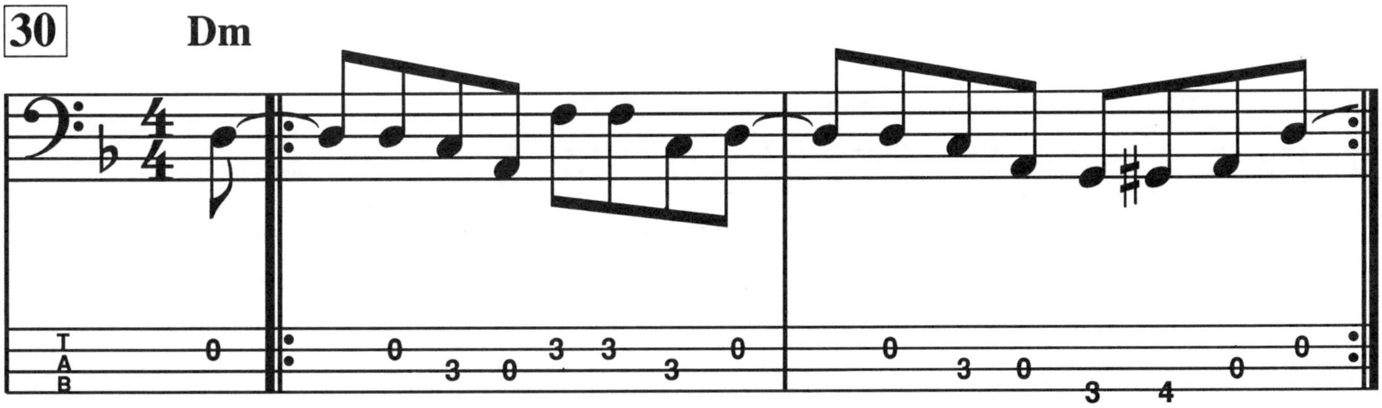

31

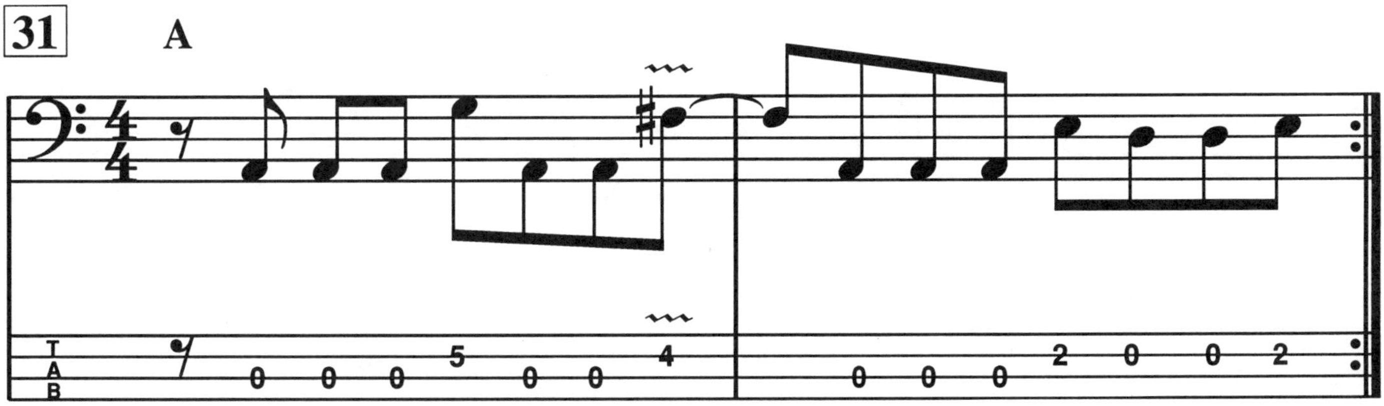

32

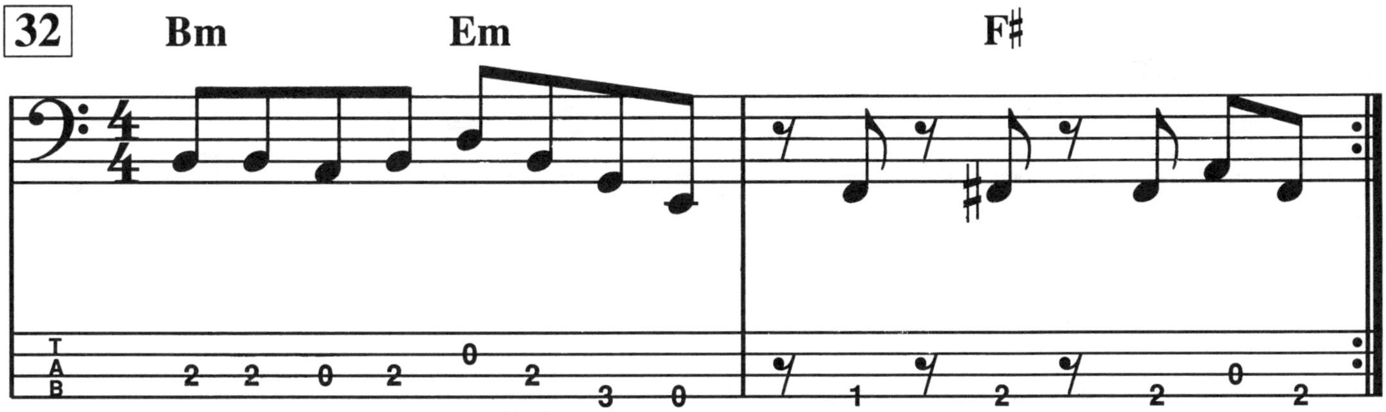

33

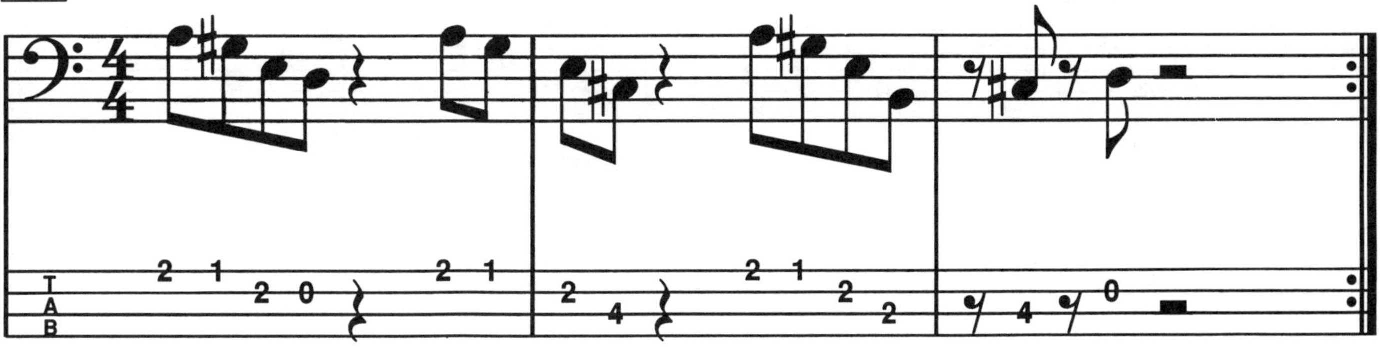

Lick 34 uses the Root note and 5th only.

34

35

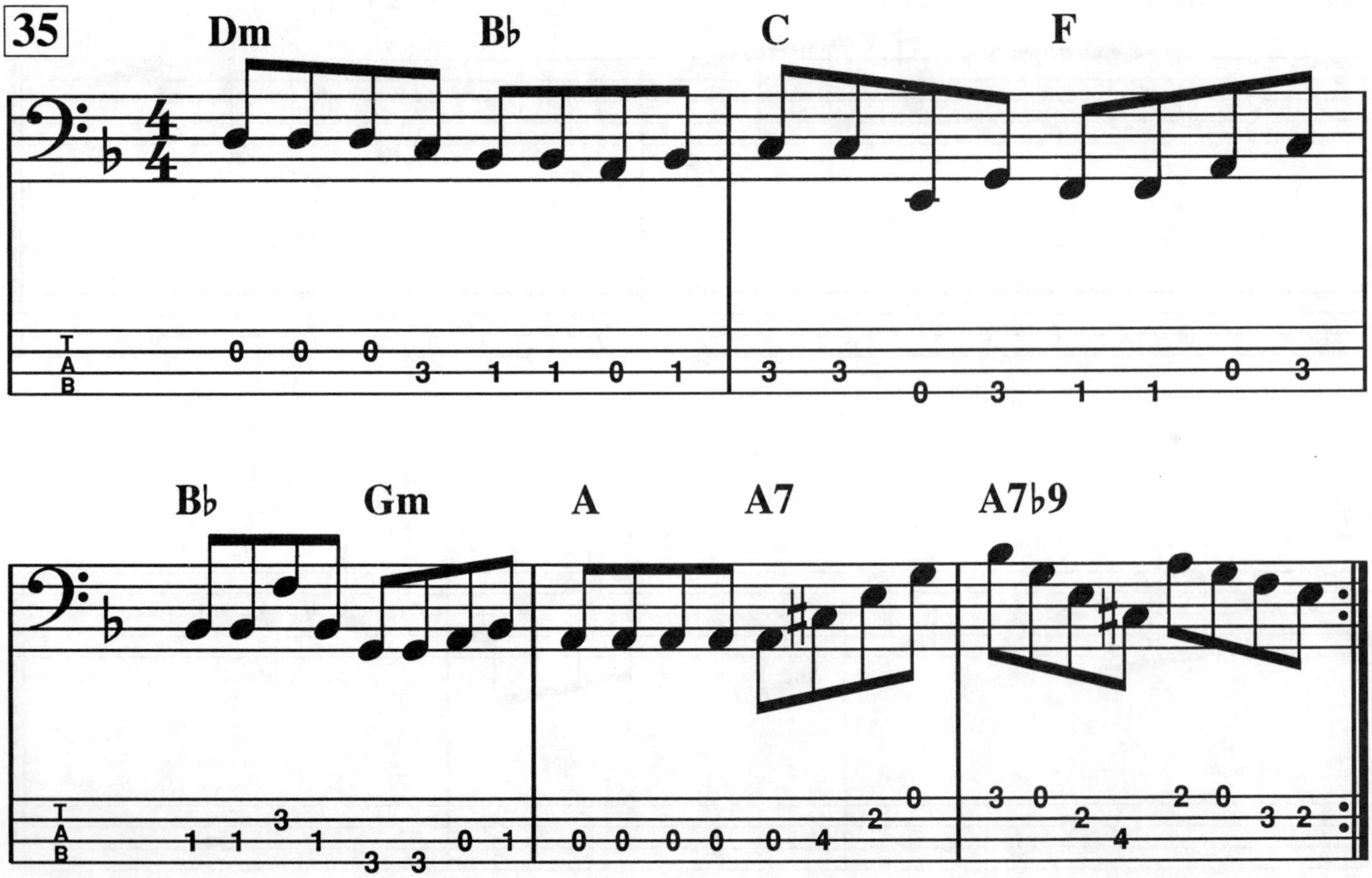

36

37

38

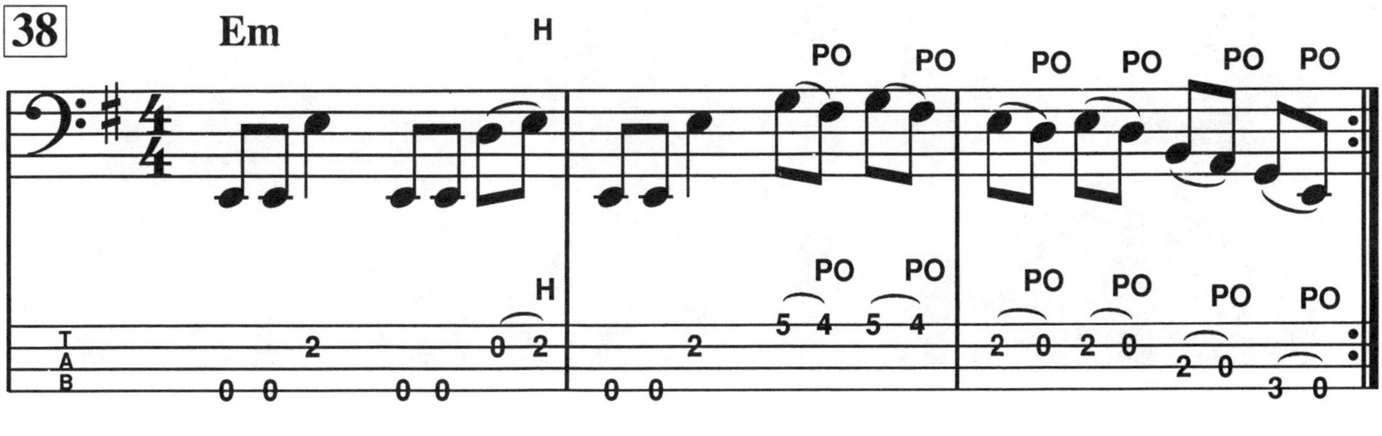

39

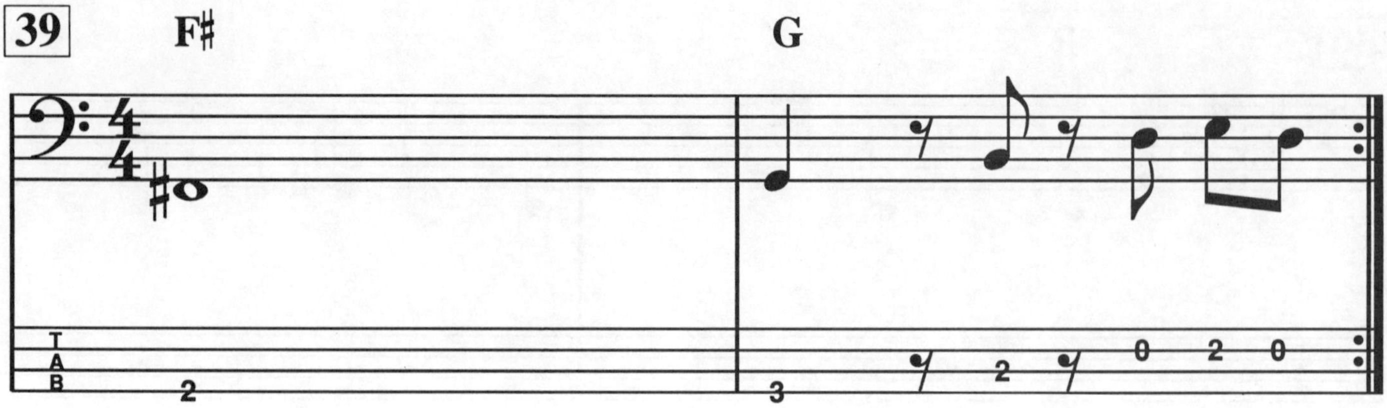

40

Bon Jovi

41

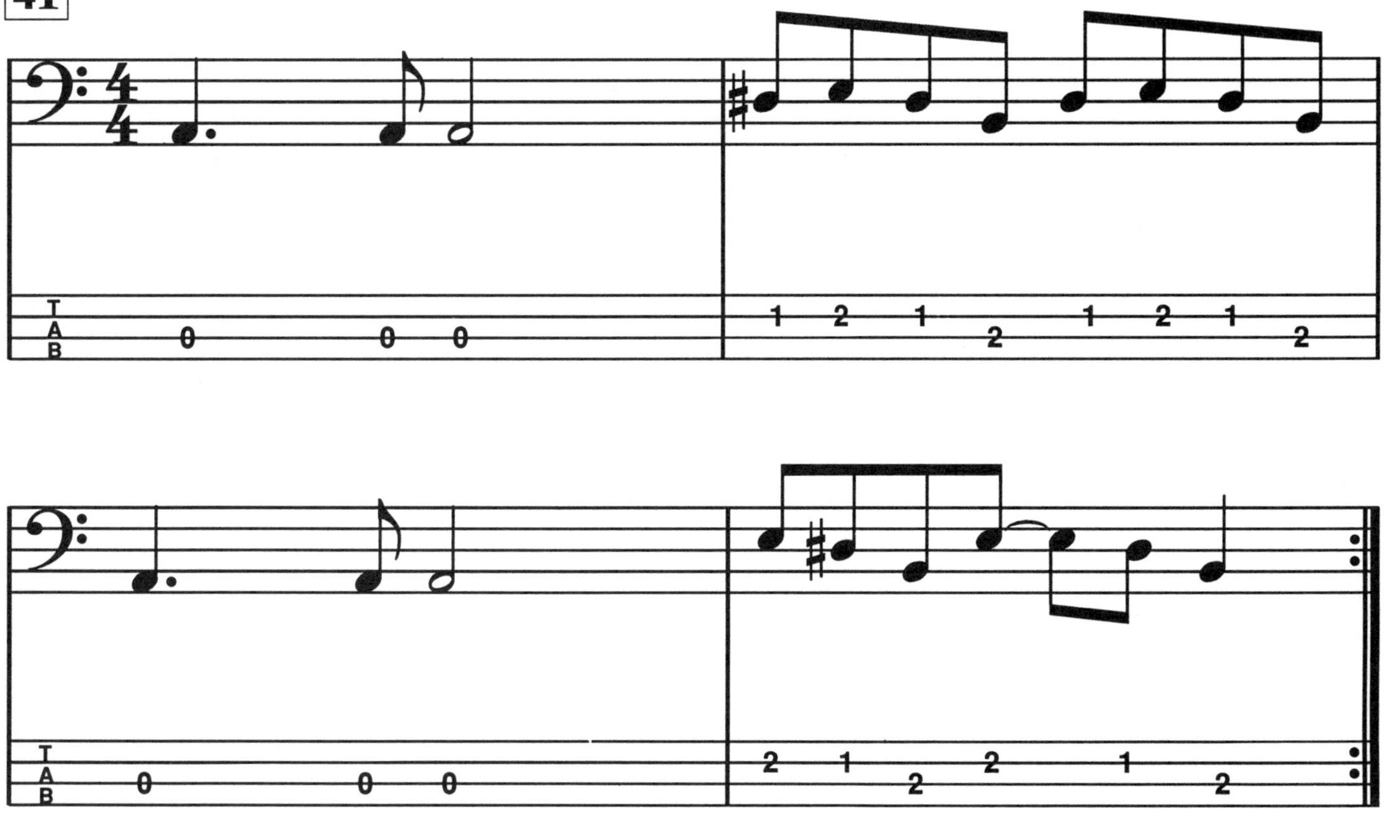

Lick 42 uses chord notes only in arpeggio style.

42

43

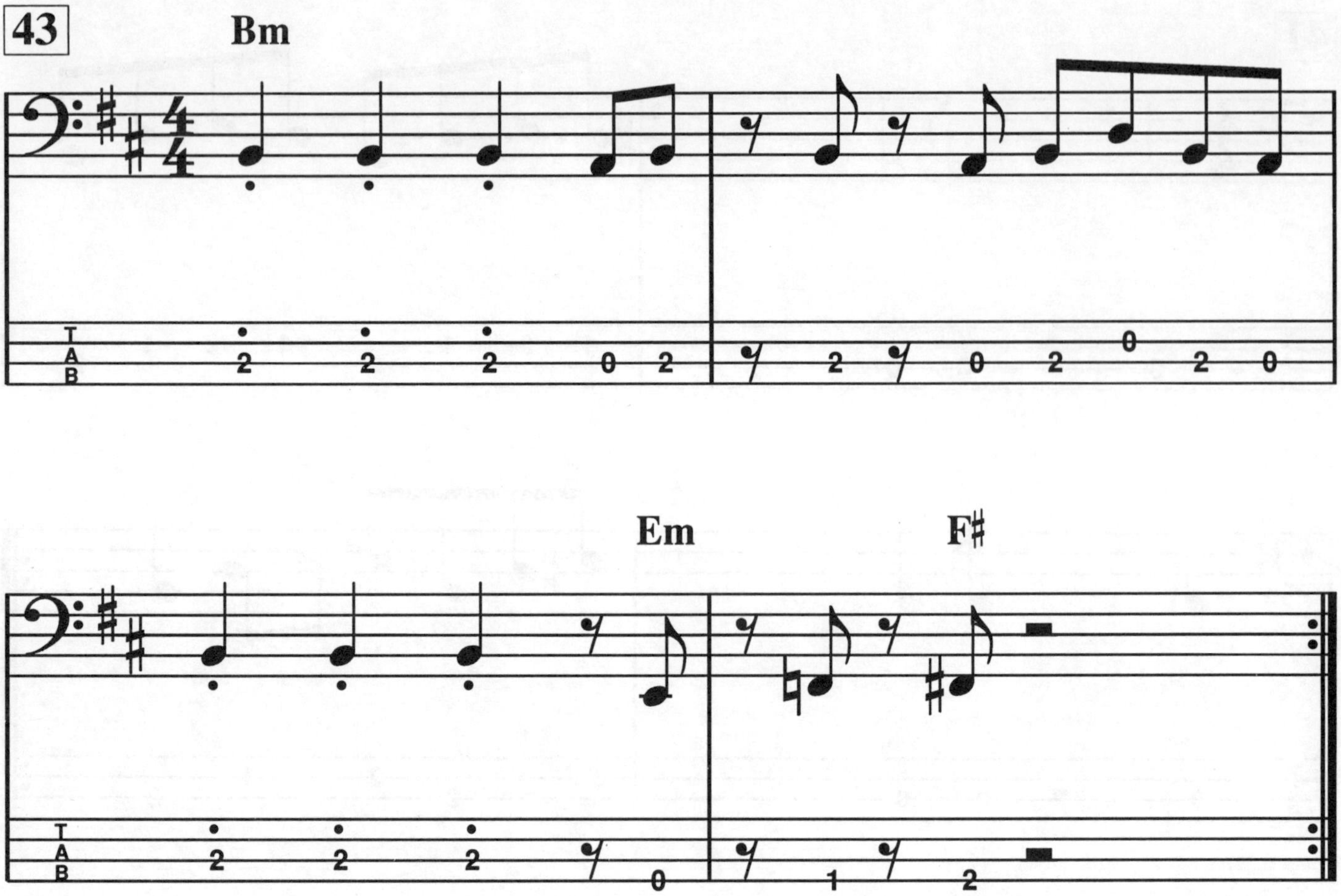

44

45

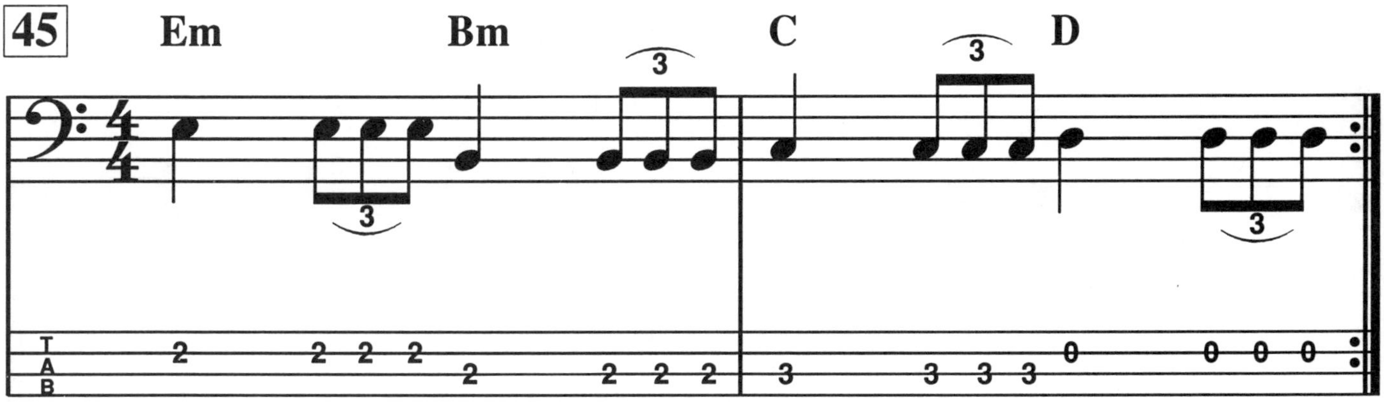

46

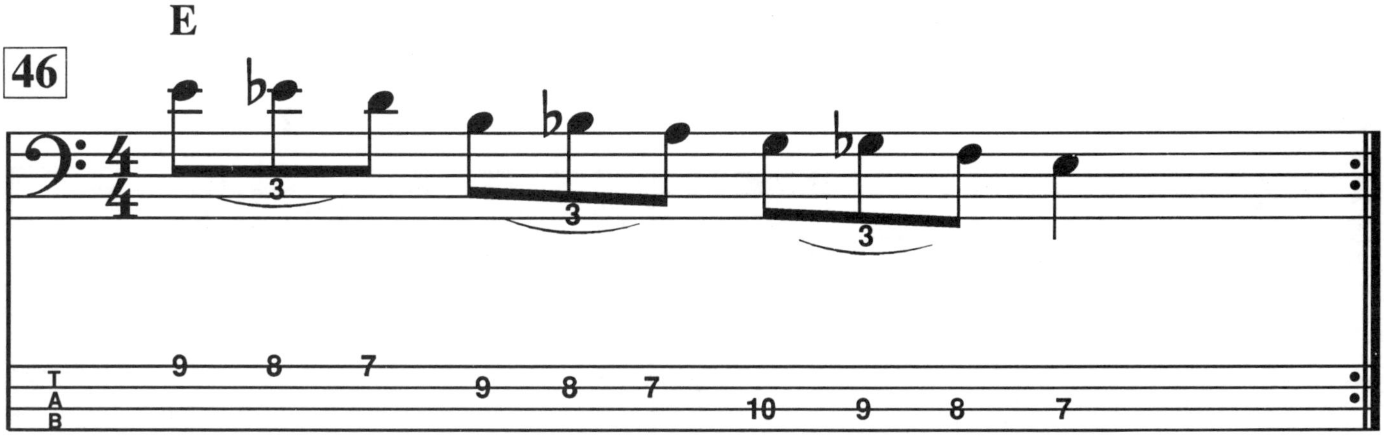

47

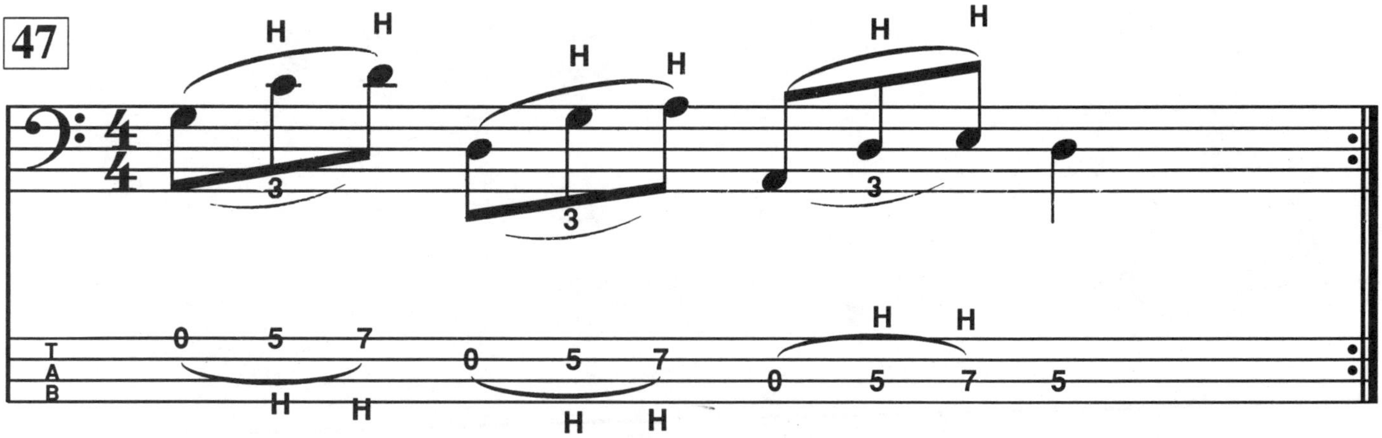

48

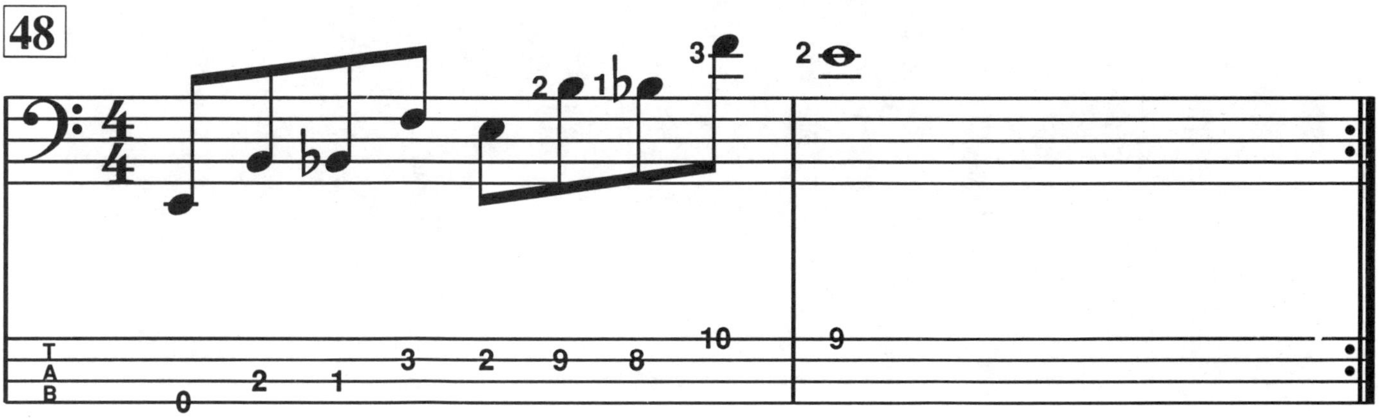

Lick 49 involves strumming chords.

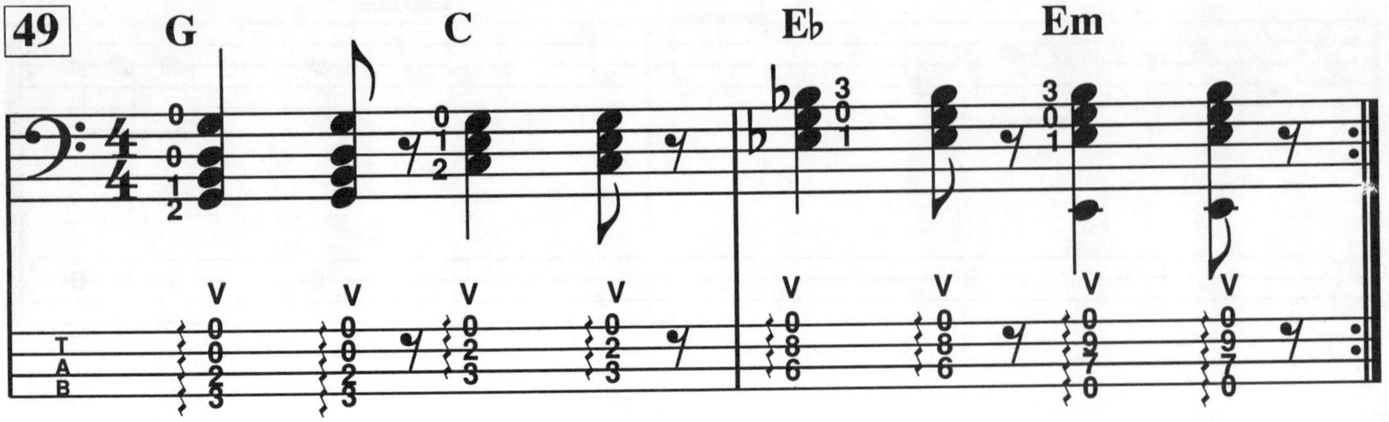

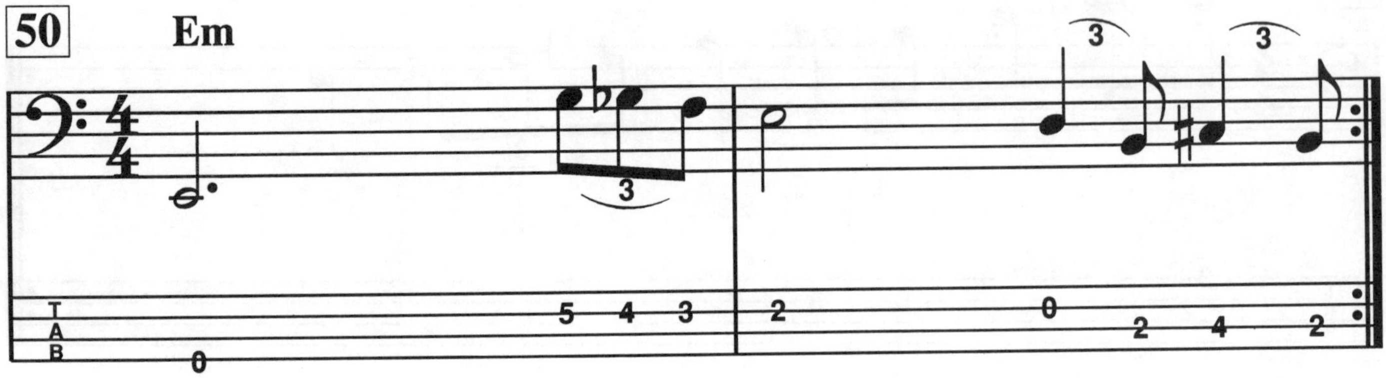

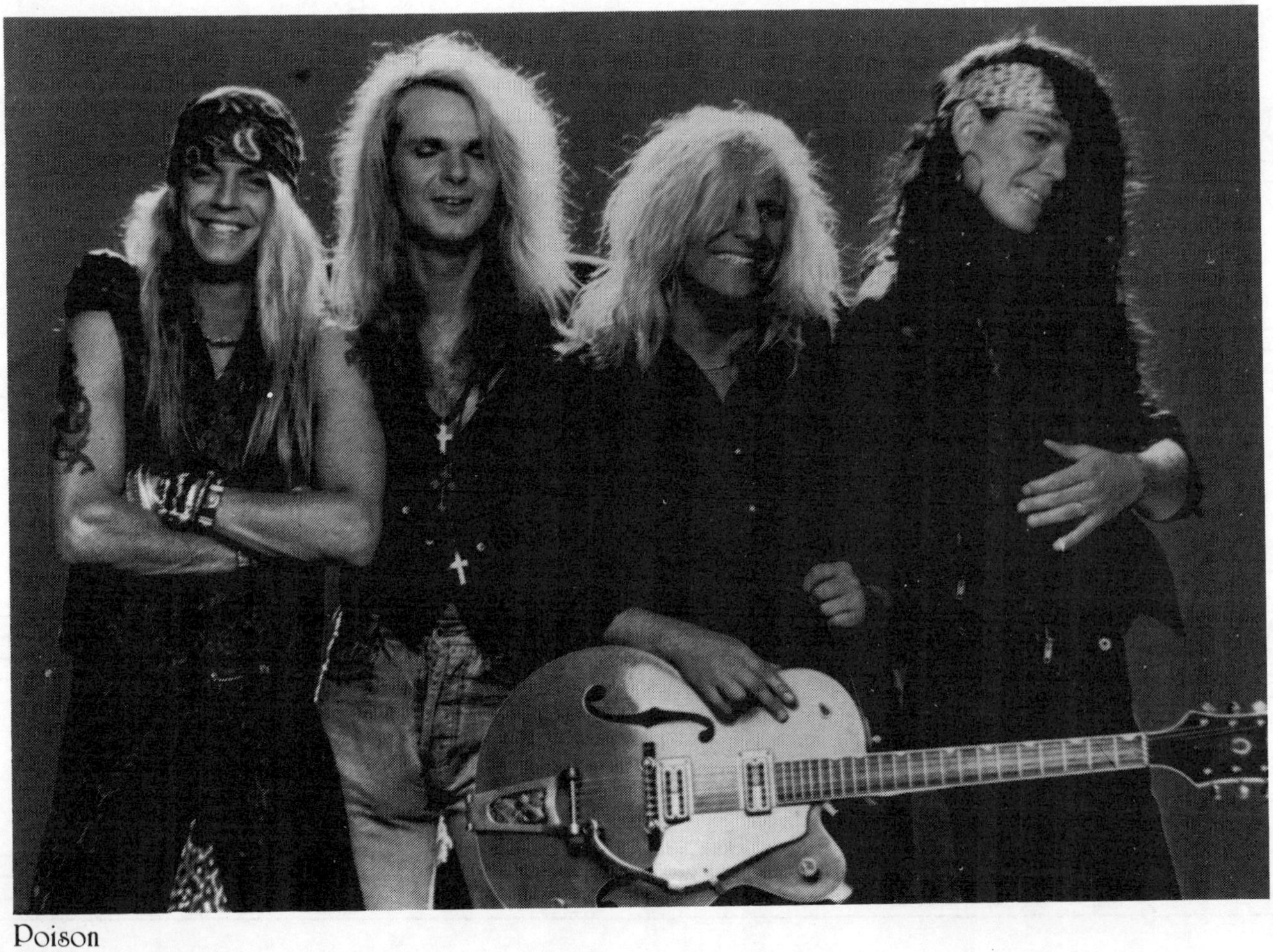

Poison

51

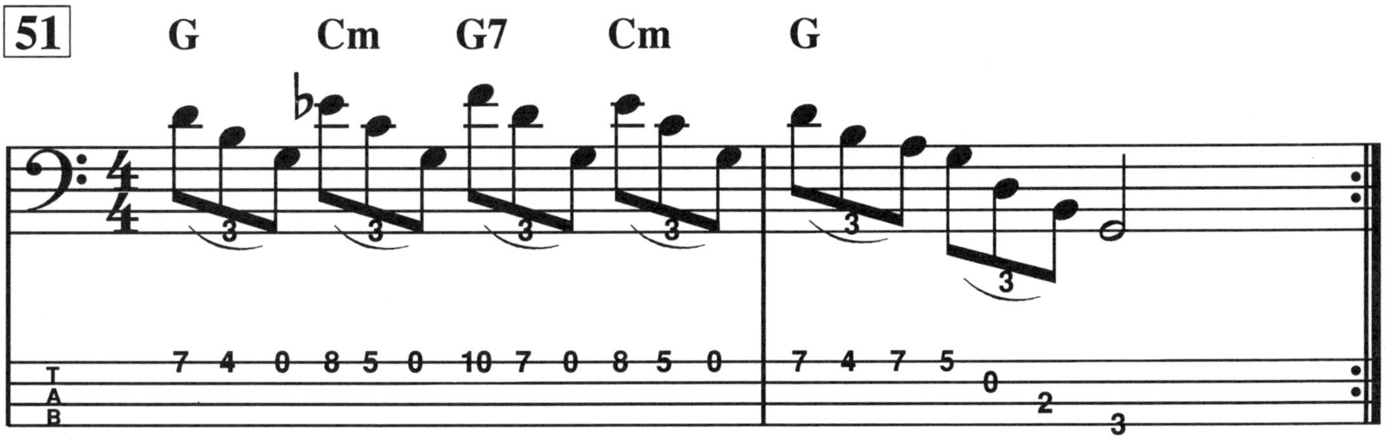
G Cm G7 Cm G
T
A
B
7 4 0 8 5 0 10 7 0 8 5 0 7 4 7 5 0 2 3

52

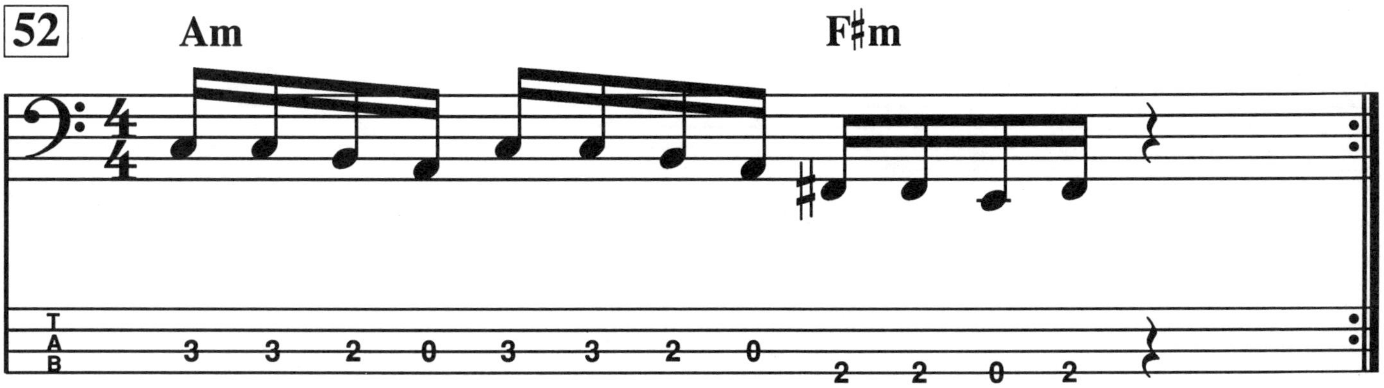
Am F♯m
T
A
B
3 3 2 0 3 3 2 0 2 2 0 2

53

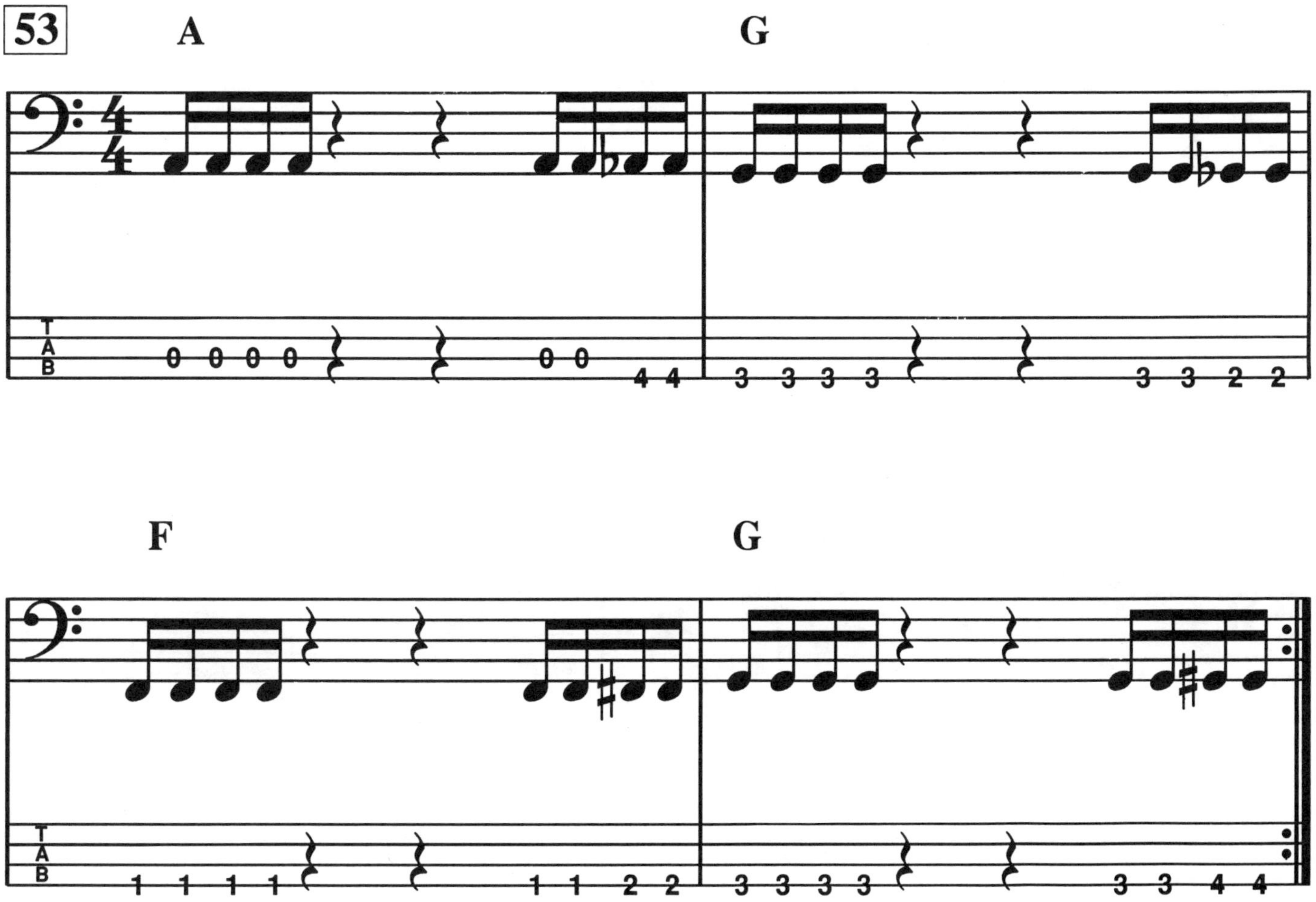
A G
T
A
B
0 0 0 0 0 0 4 4 3 3 3 3 3 3 2 2
F G
T
A
B
1 1 1 1 1 1 2 2 3 3 3 3 3 3 4 4

54

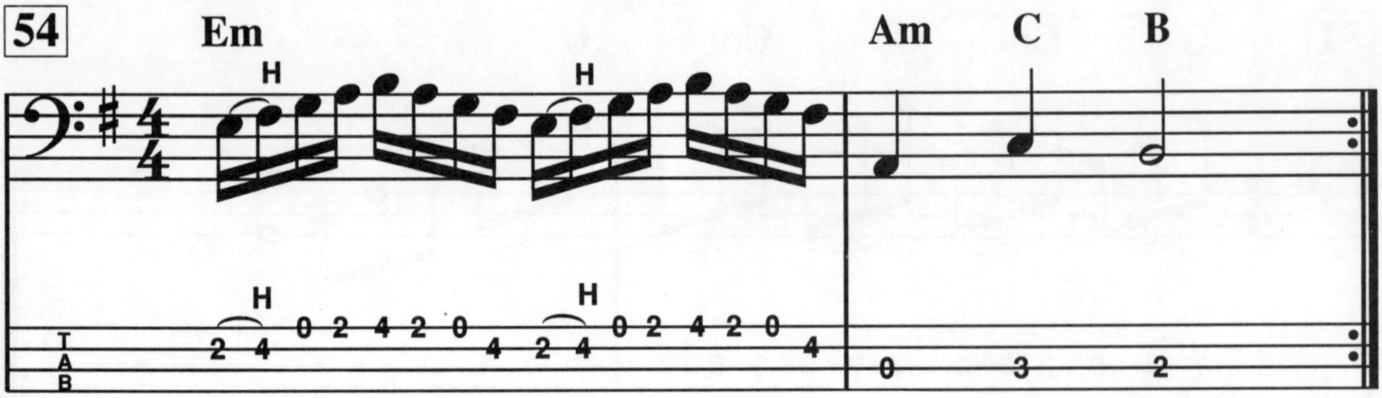

55

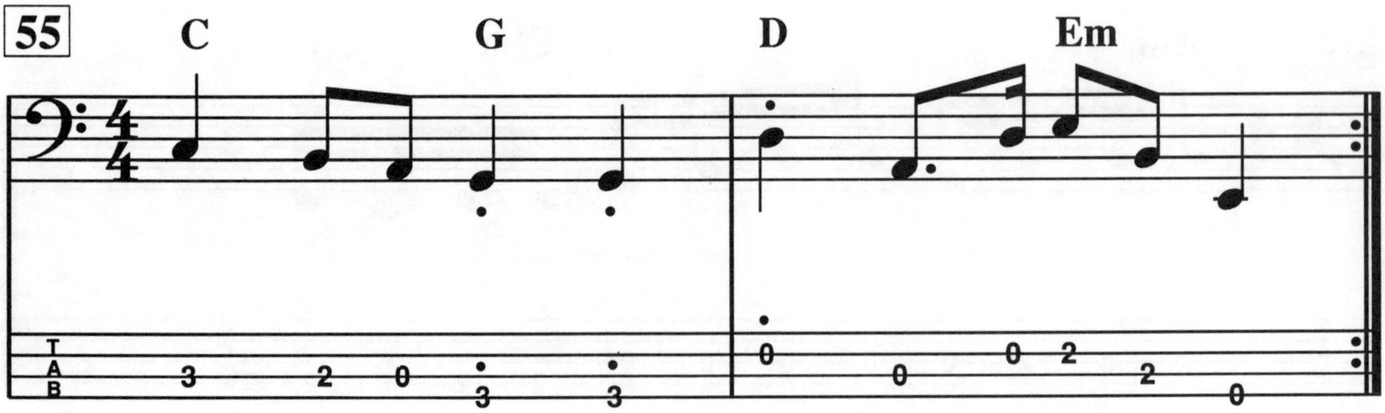

56

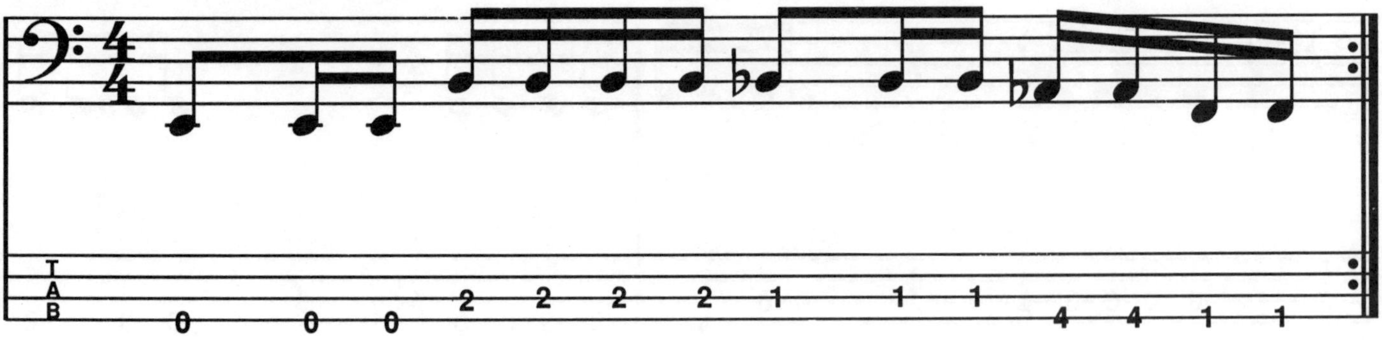

57

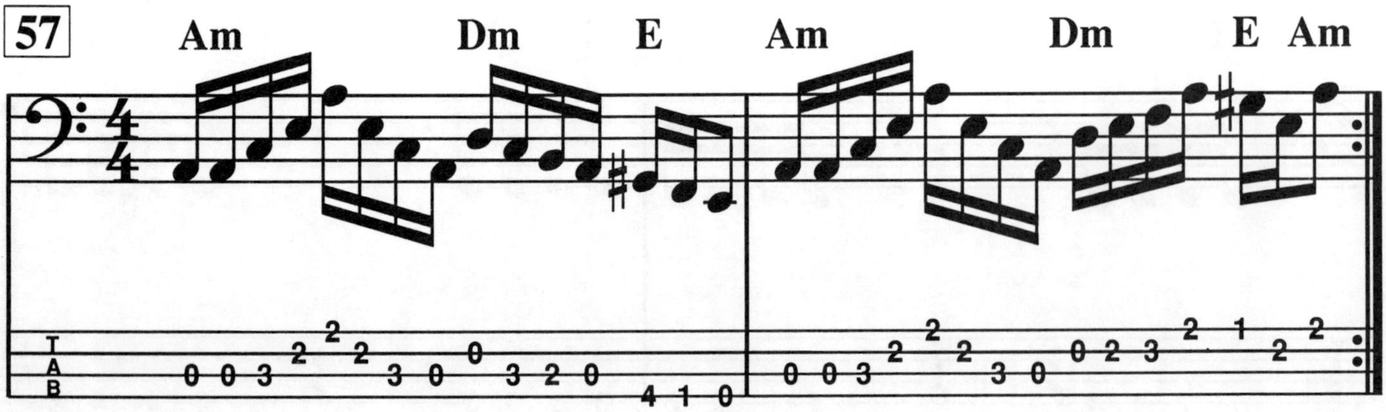

58

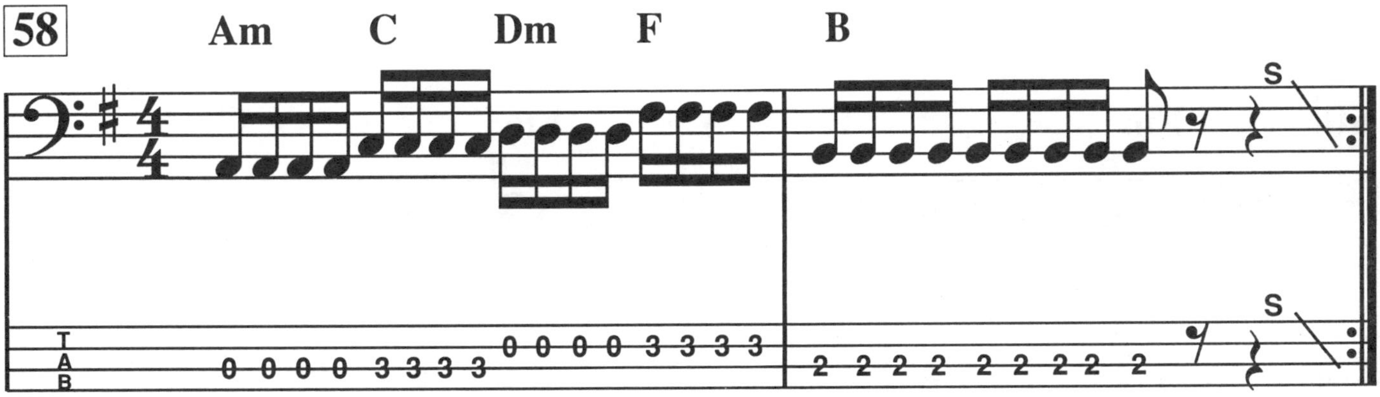

59

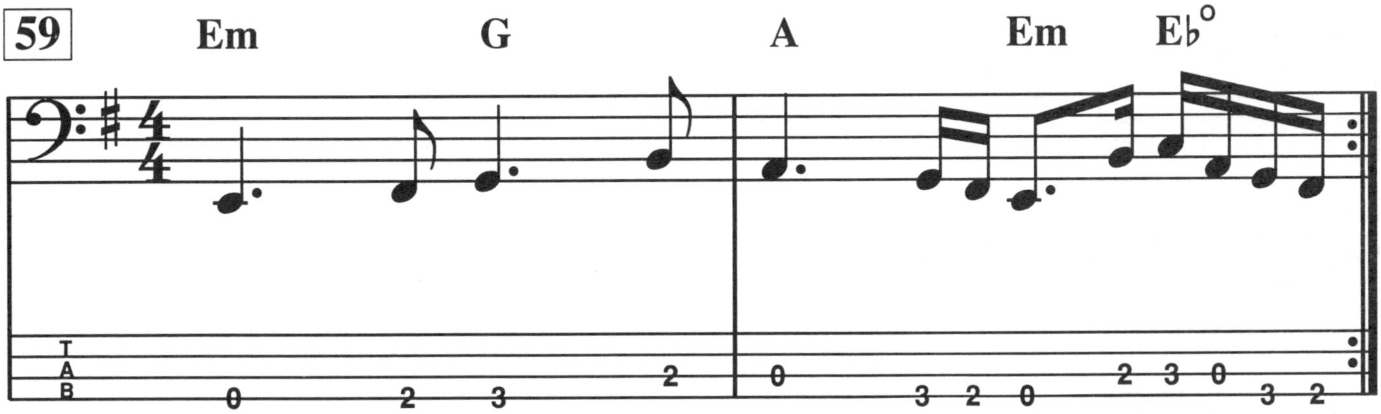

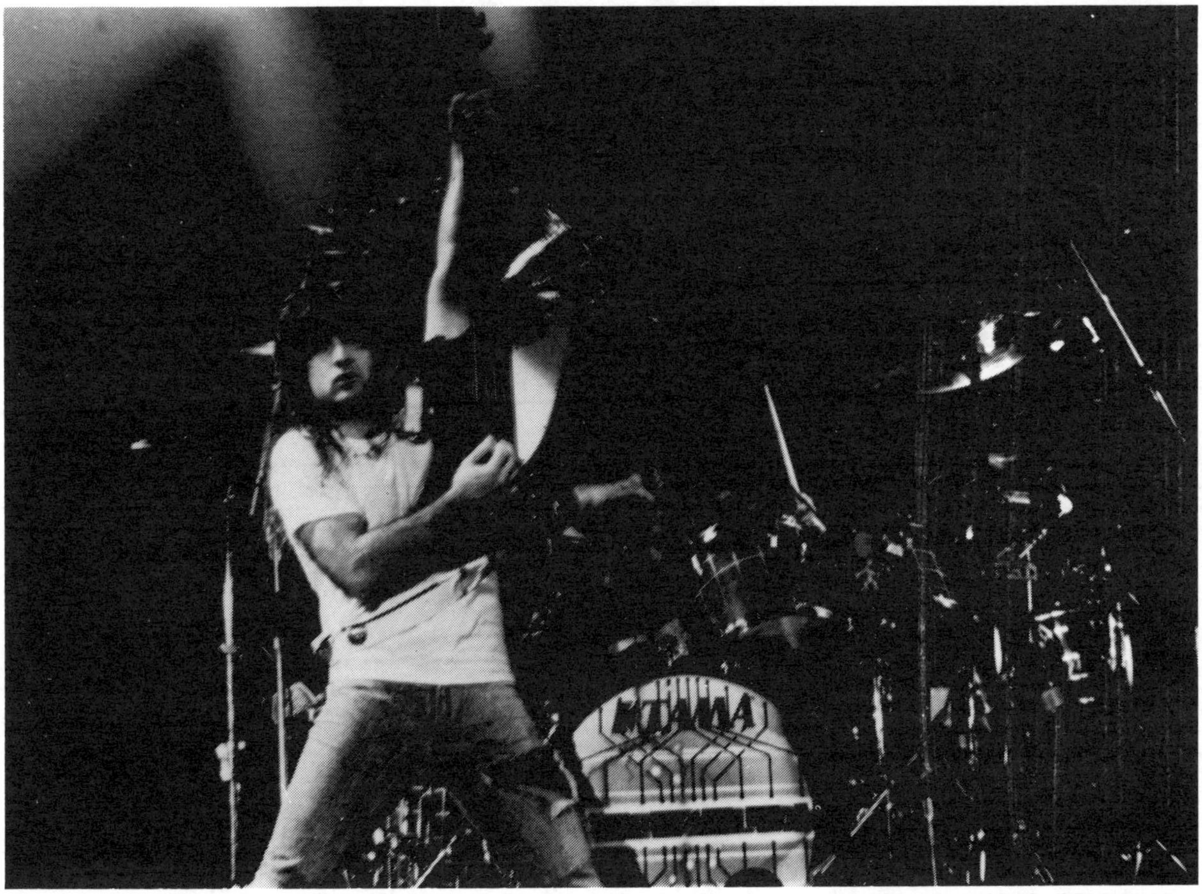

Francis Buchholz (Scorpions)

This lick is in $\frac{6}{8}$ time. Listen to the tape to make sure that your timing is correct.

The next four licks can be transposed onto different strings.
Use pick or fingers for this lick.

61

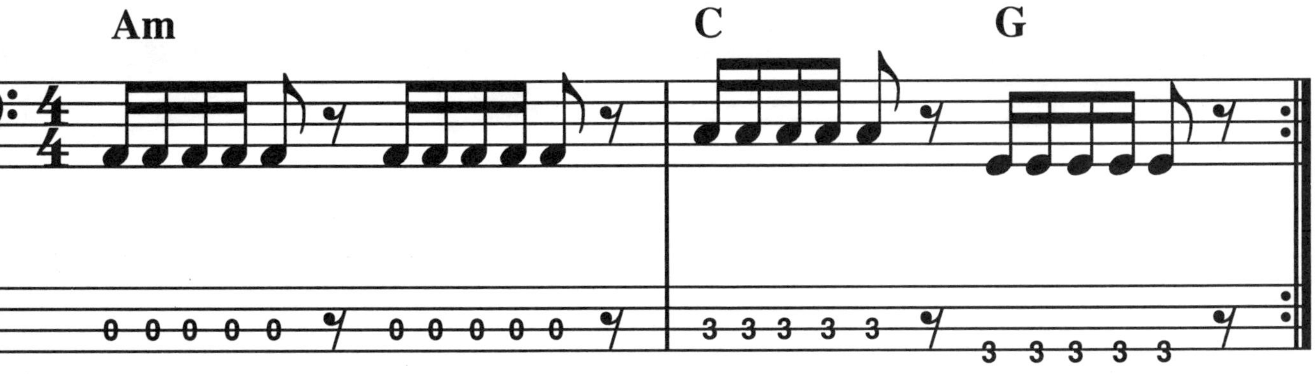

Use pick or fingers for this lick.

62

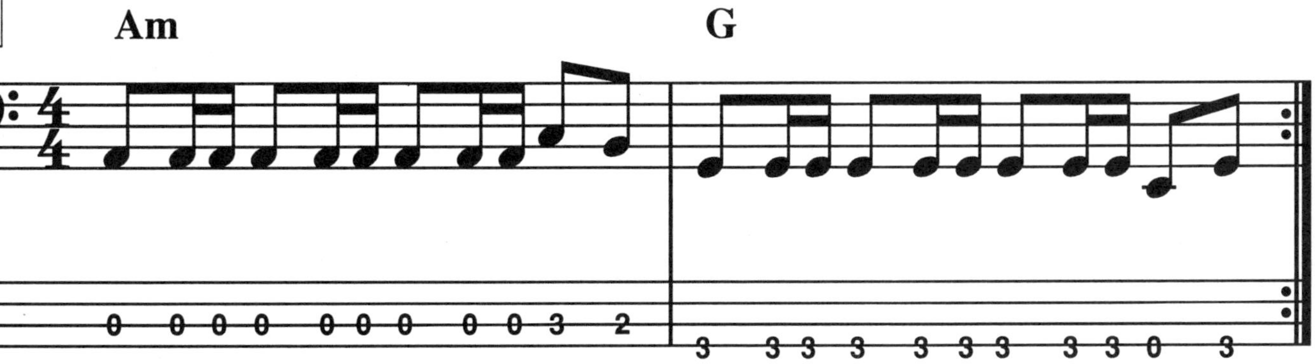

Use the pick for this lick.

63

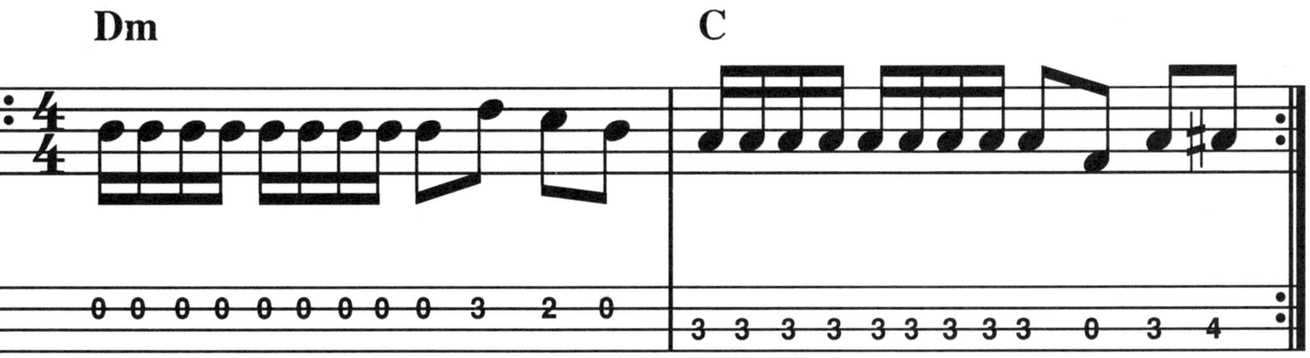

64

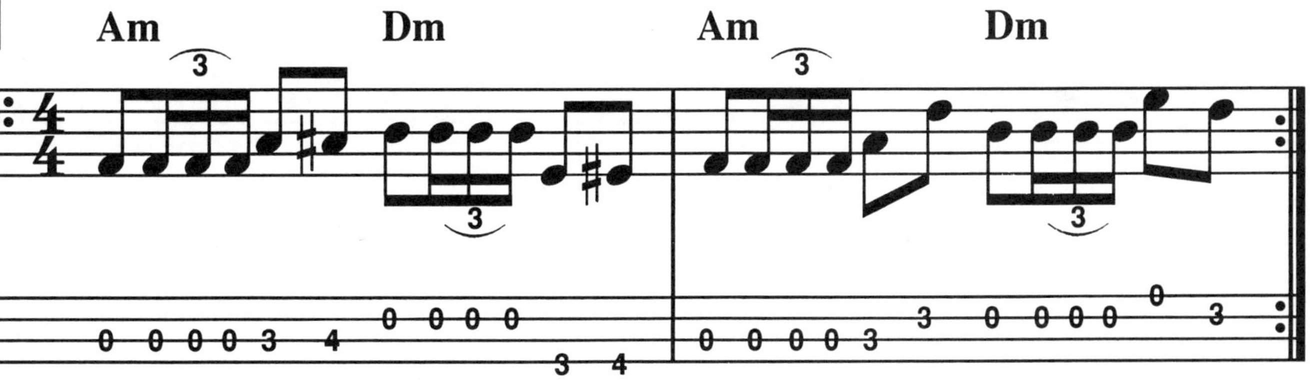

Lick 65 is played very fast using a pick. It is an example of speed metal.

65

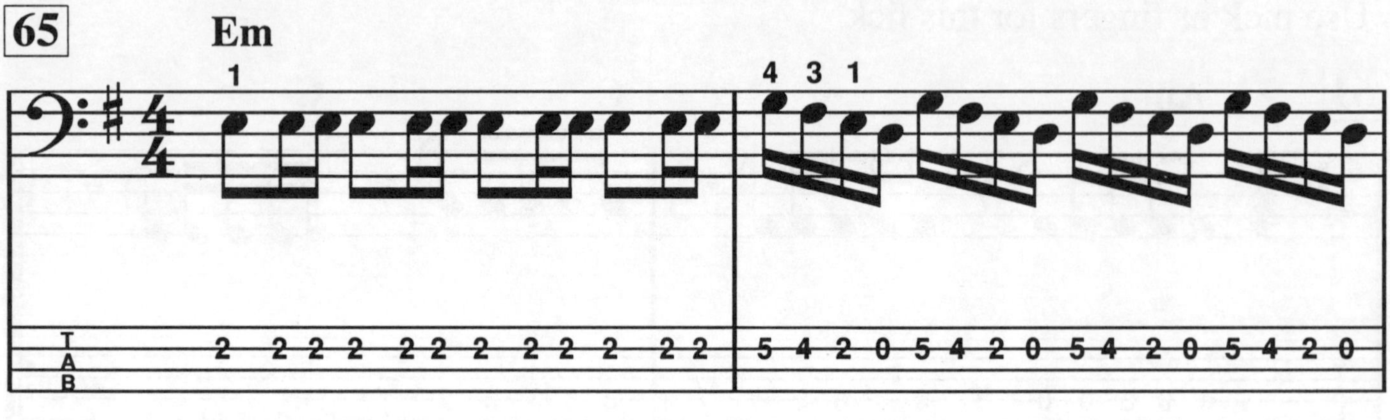

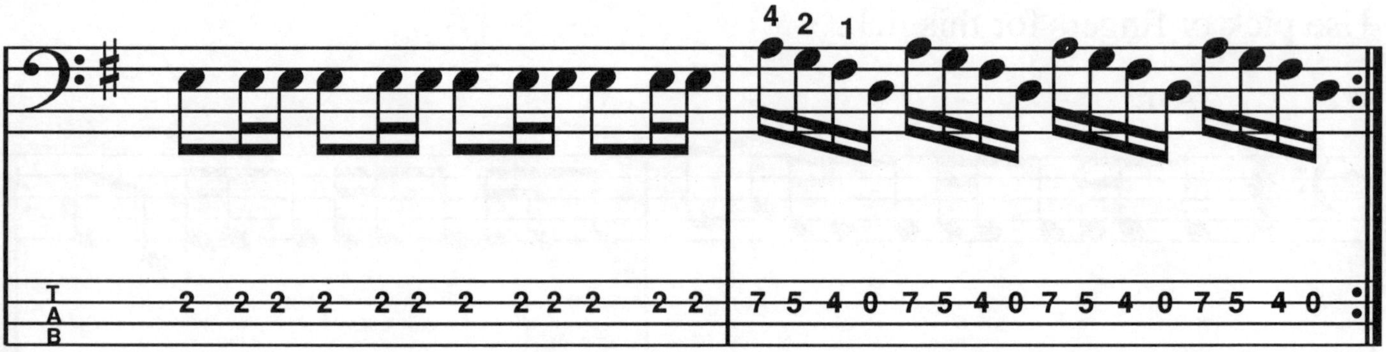

Lick 66 is in $\frac{6}{4}$ time. Use the pick or fingers.

66

67

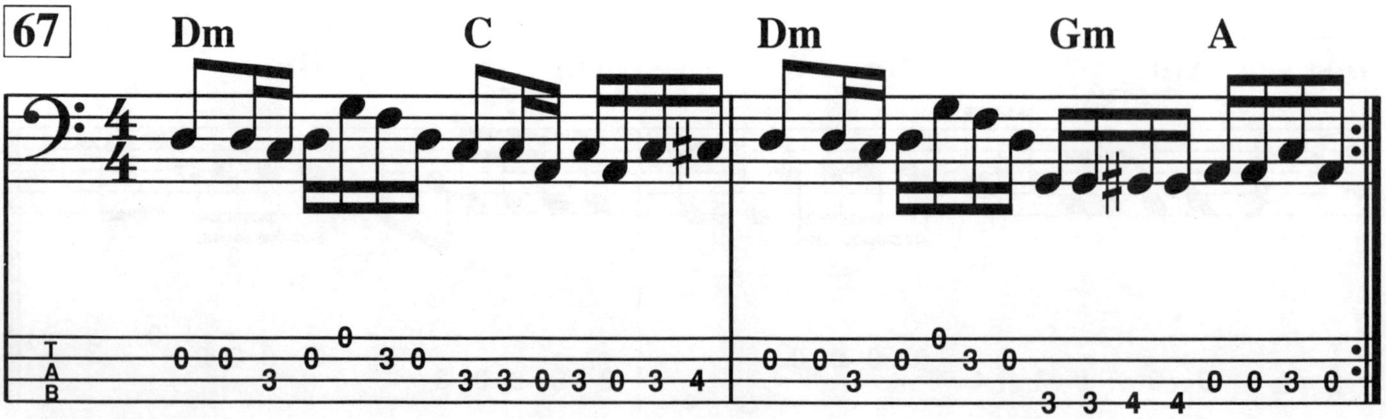

68

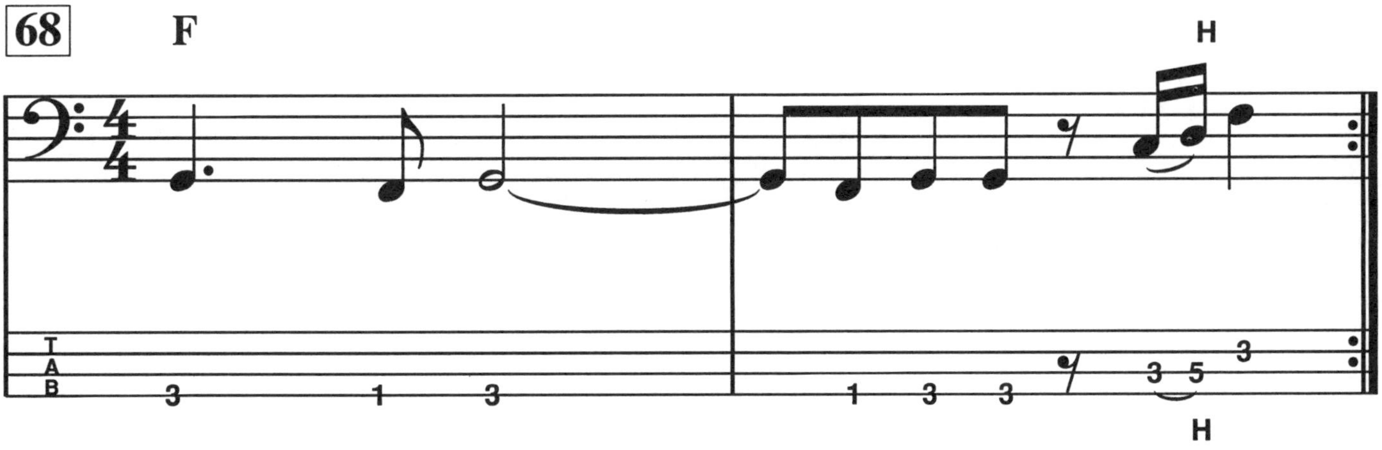

Lick 69 is in $\frac{6}{4}$ time.

69

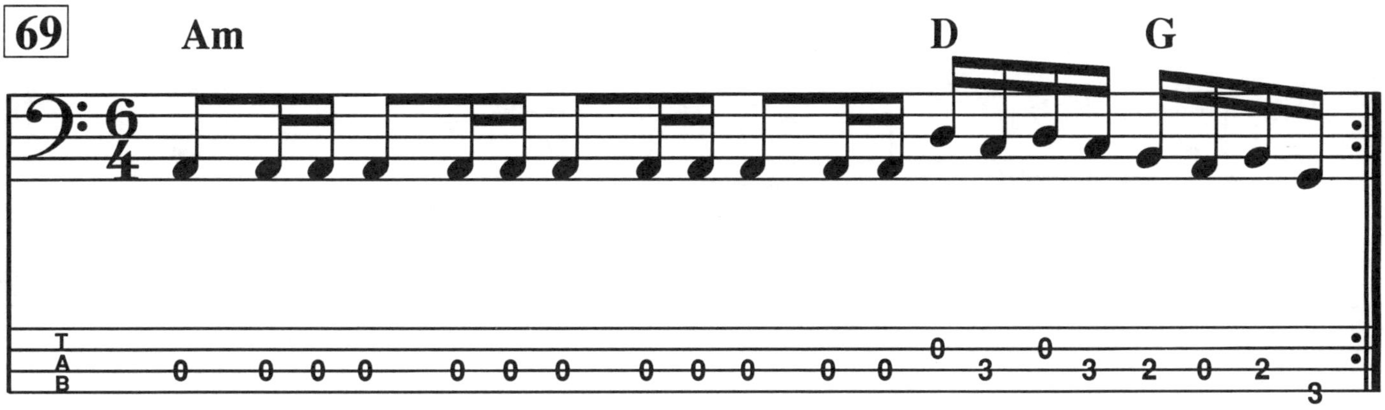

70

Lick 71 uses power chords in the second bar.

71

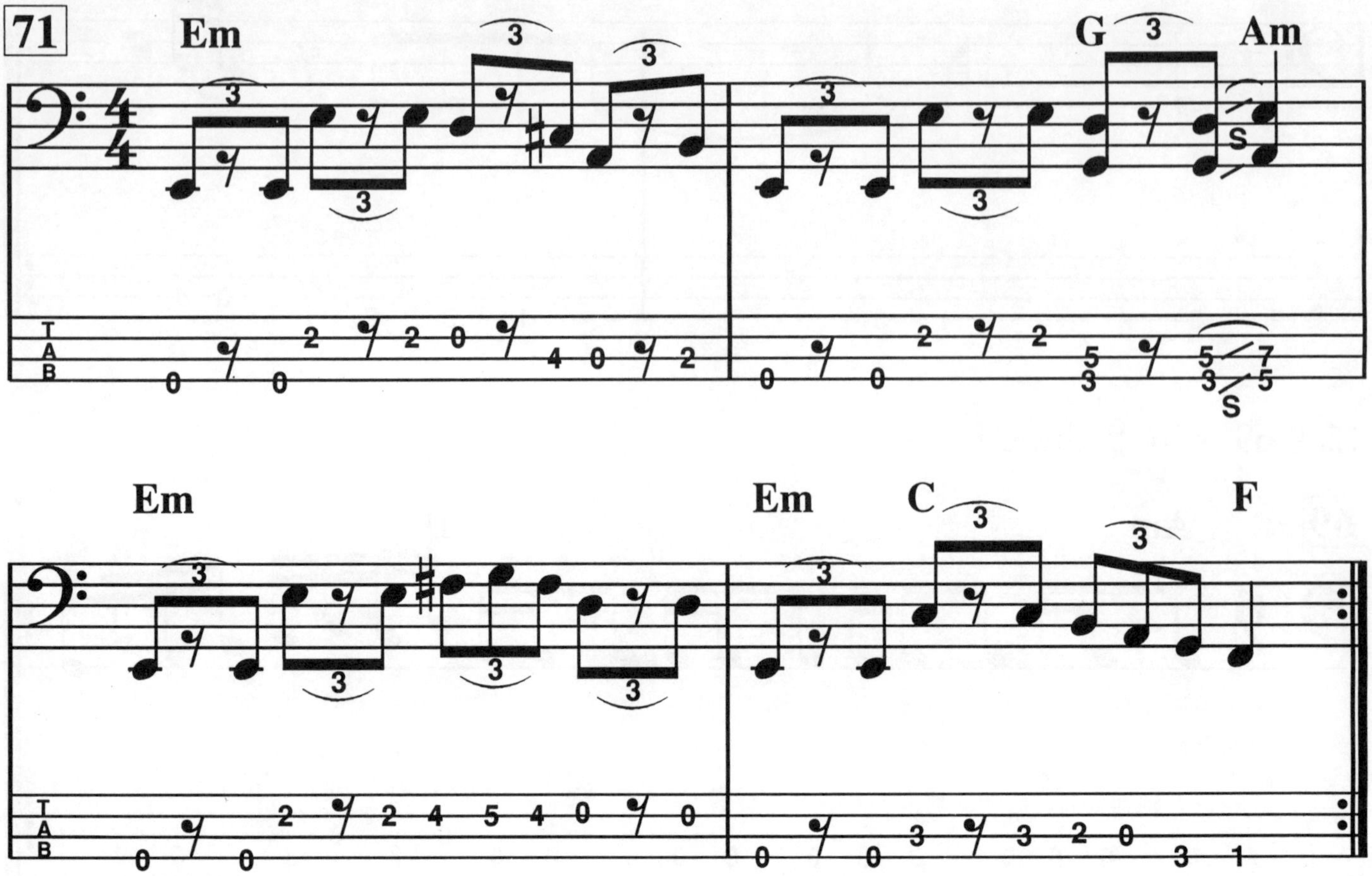

72

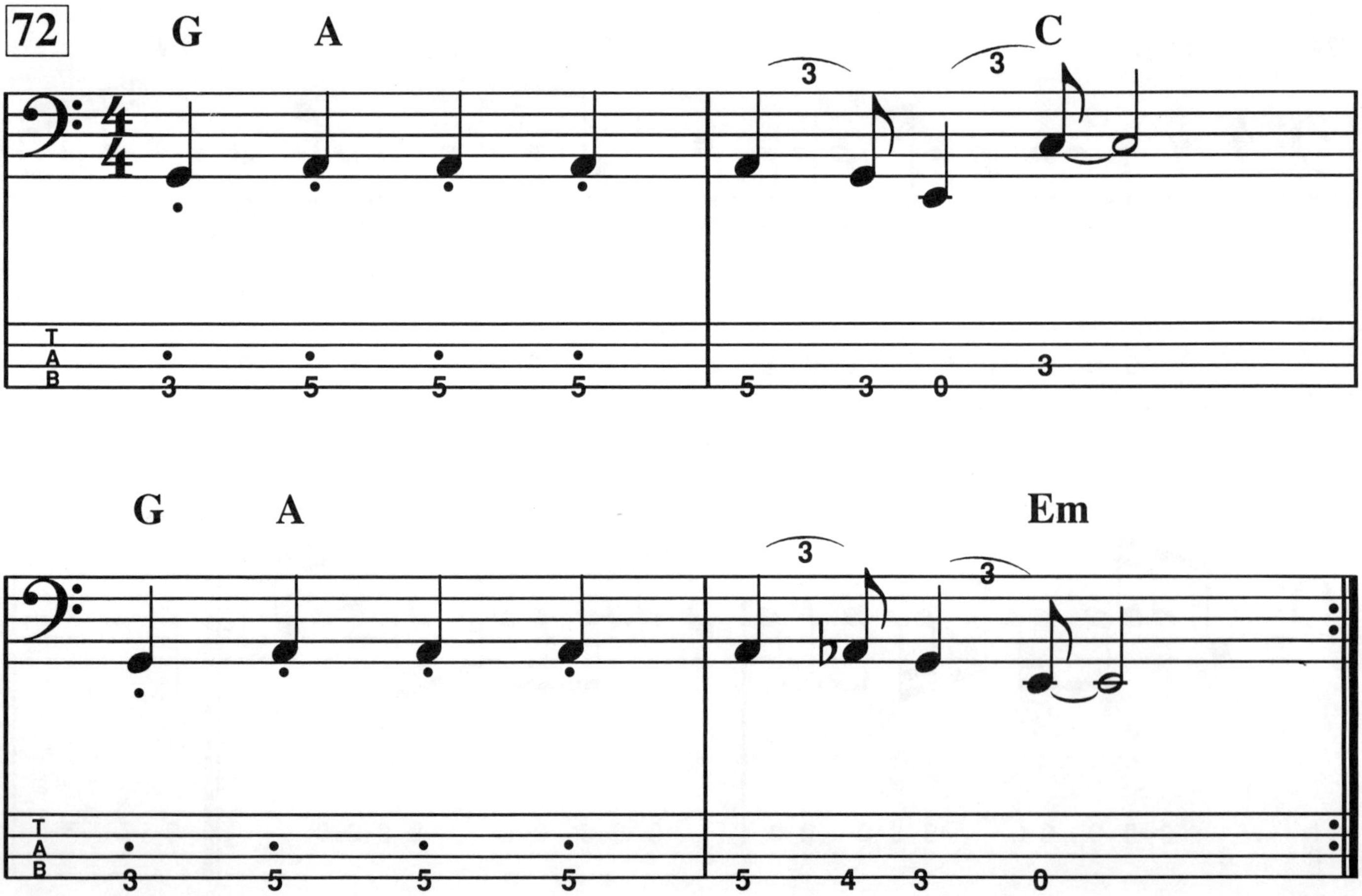

73

74

75

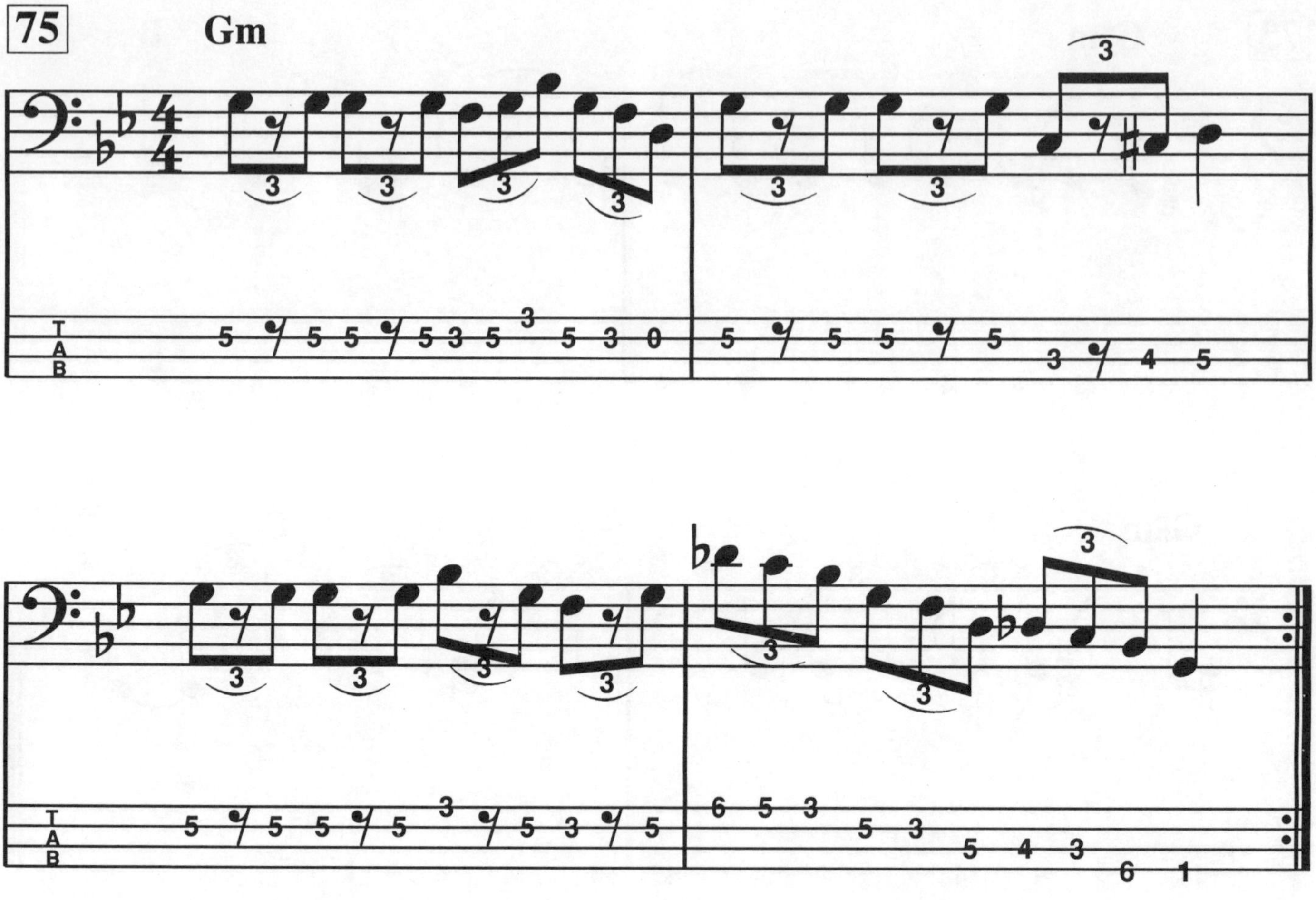

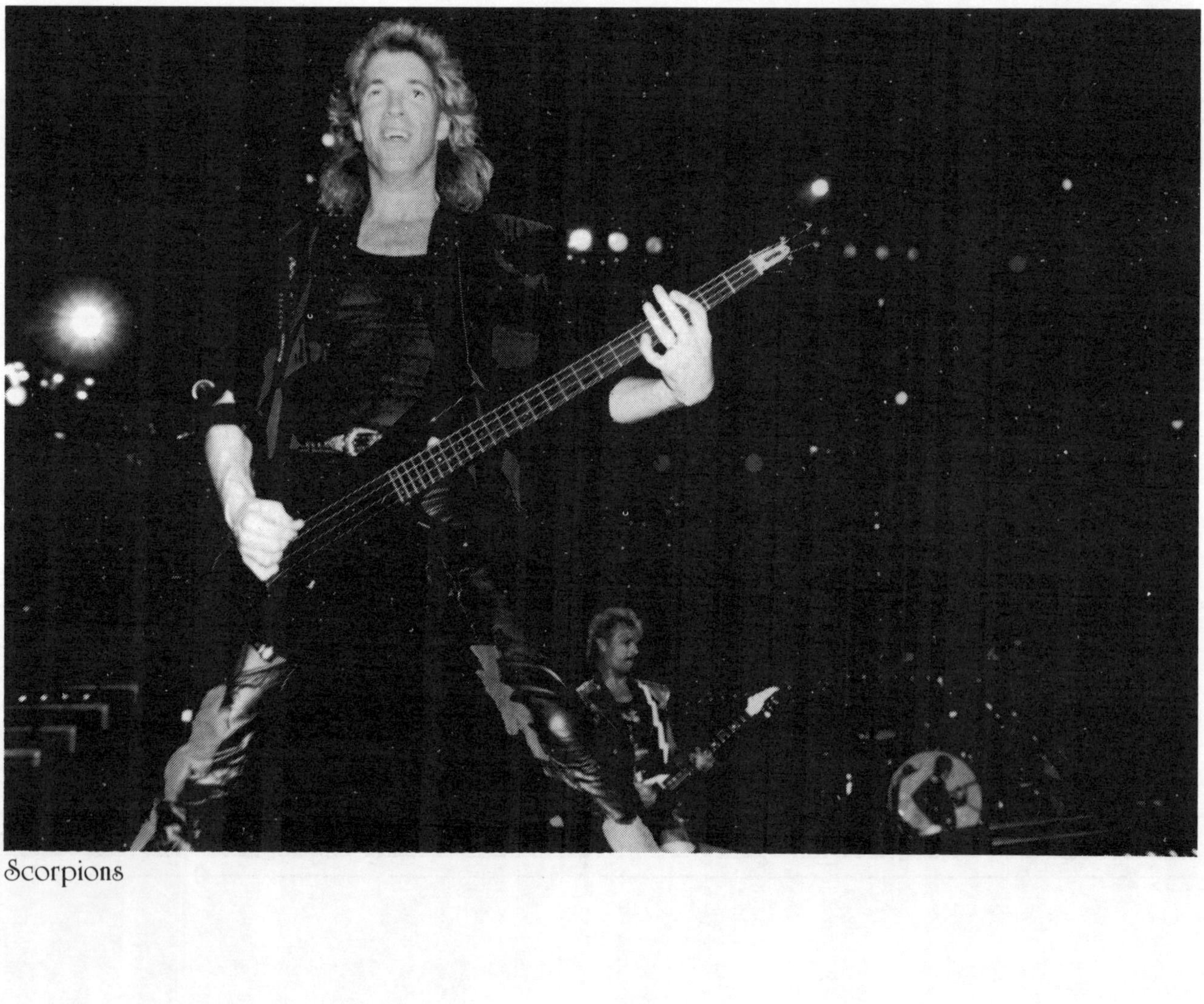

Scorpions

76

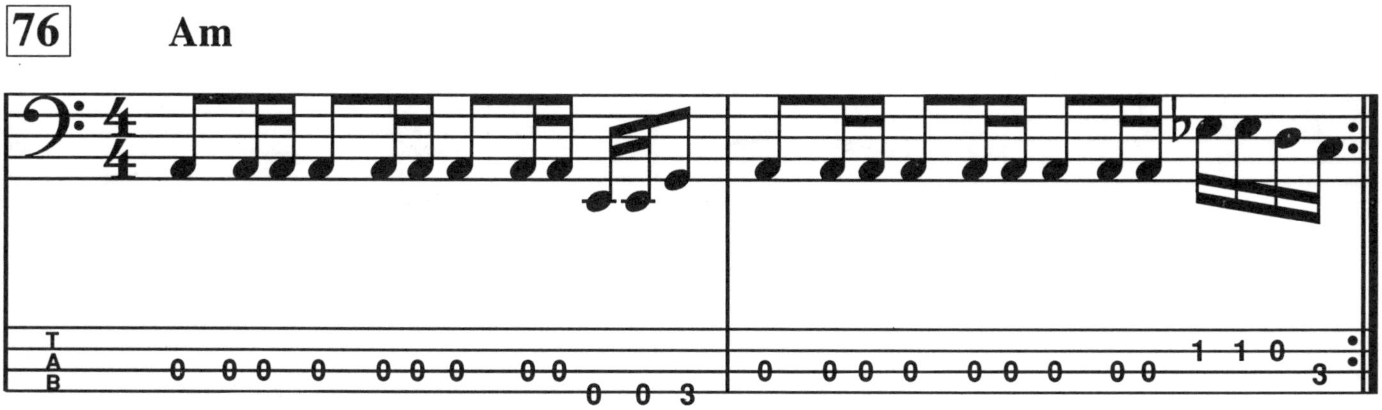

77

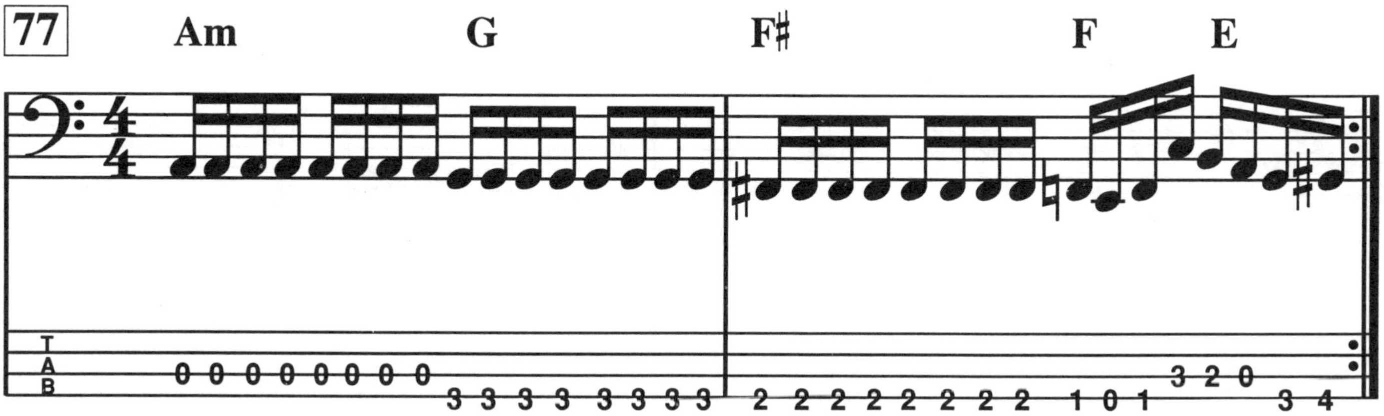

78

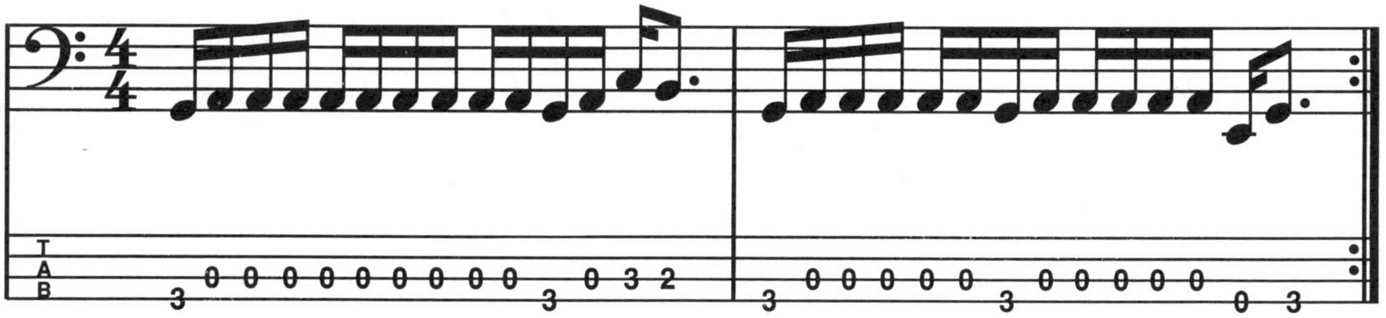

Lick 79 is based upon the E harmonic minor scale.

79

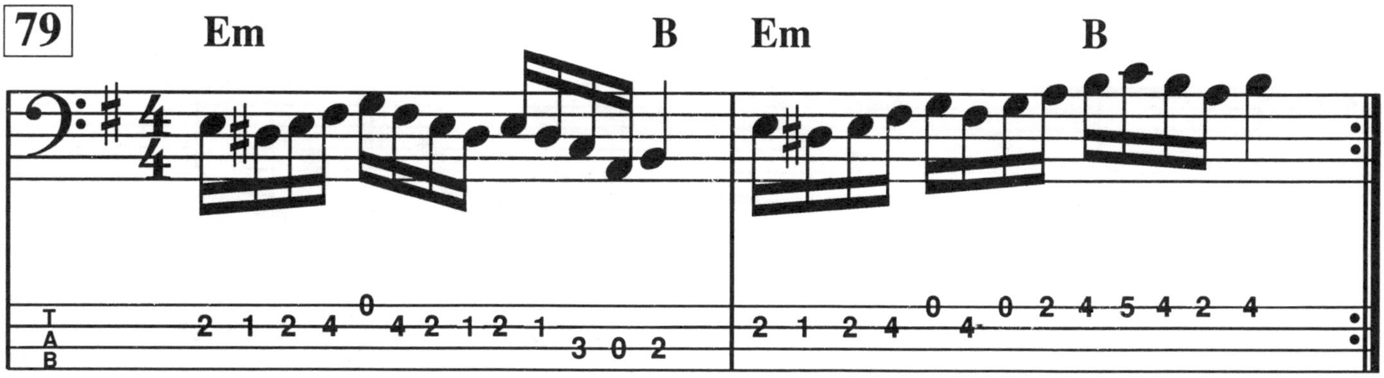

80

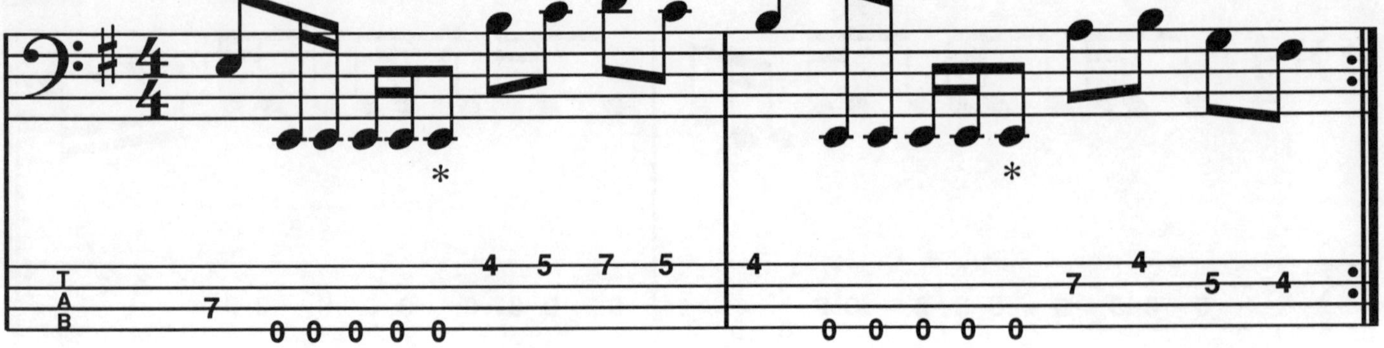

*Let these notes ring.

81

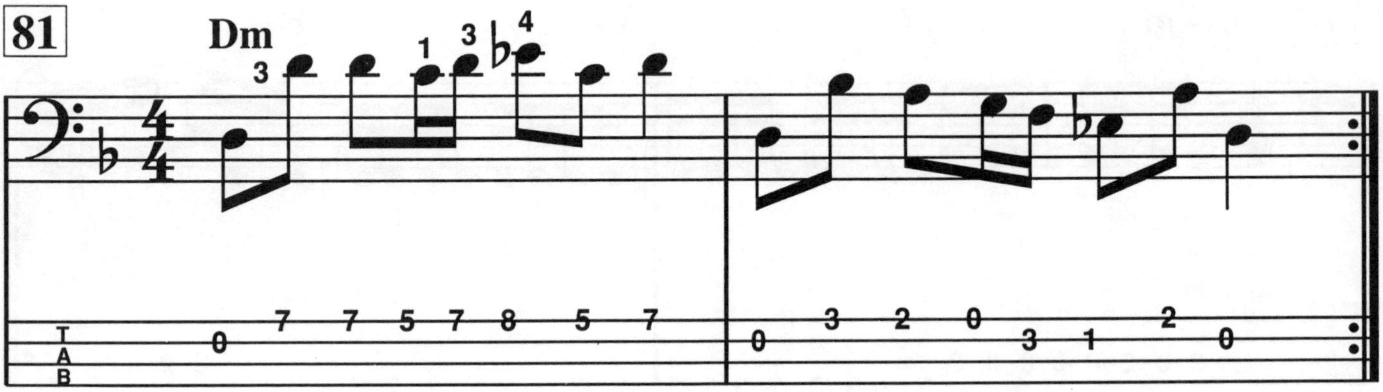

82

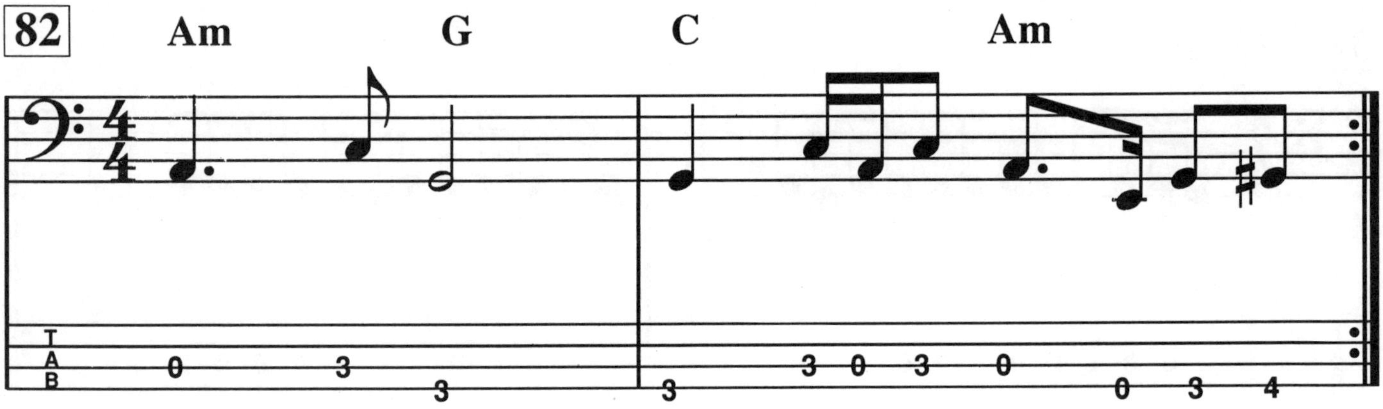

This lick ends with a sliding double stop.

83

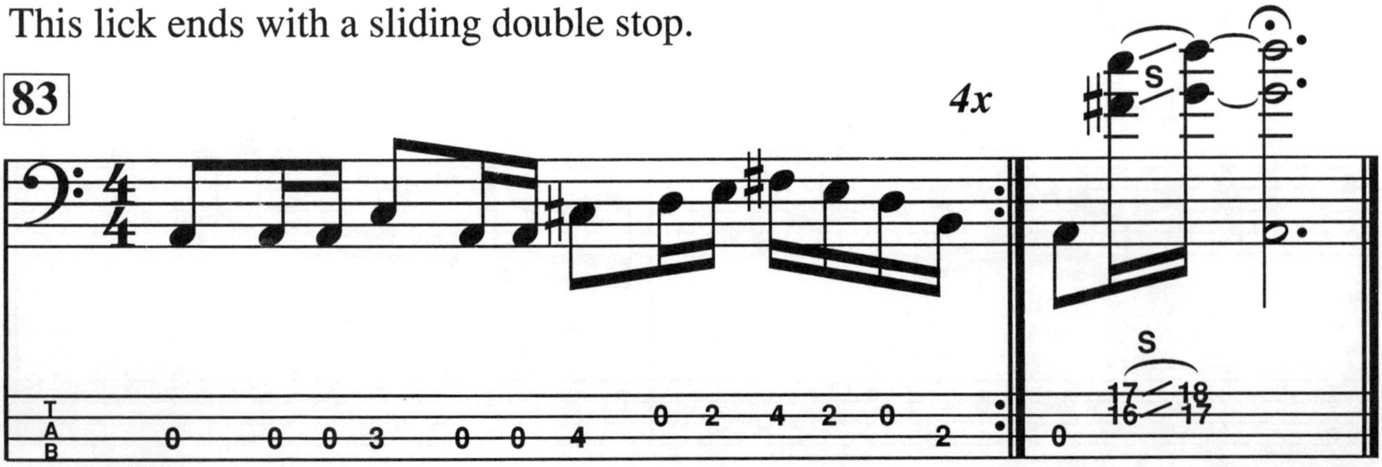

84

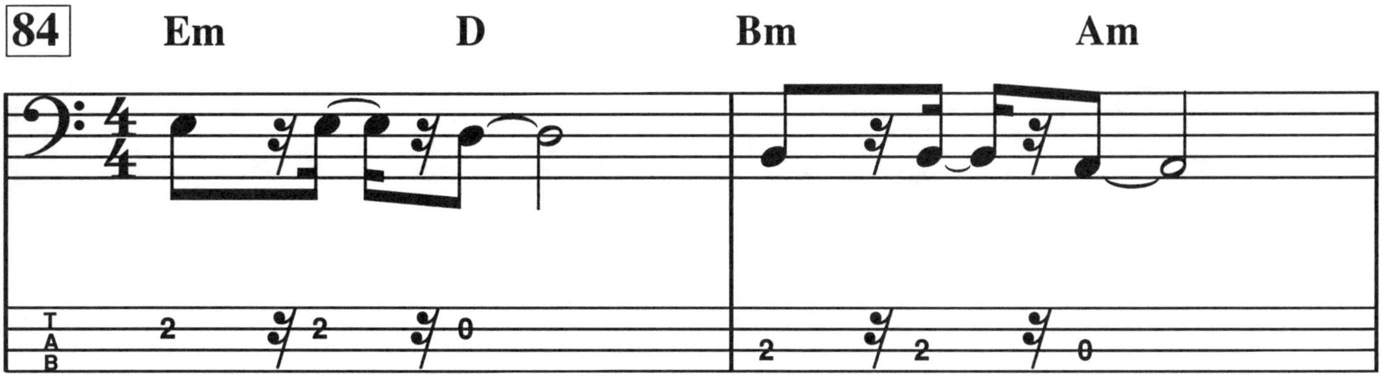

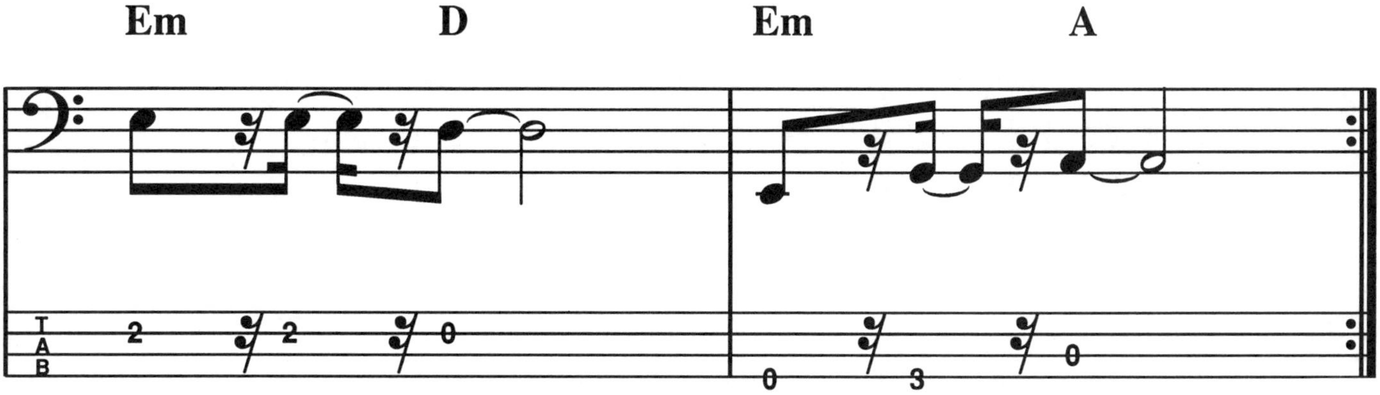

This lick is a fill in Em.

85

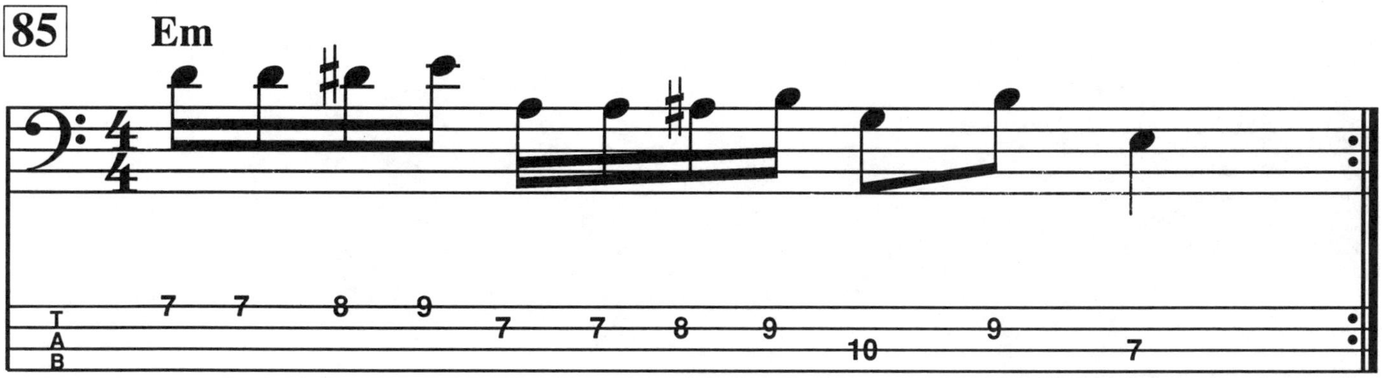

86

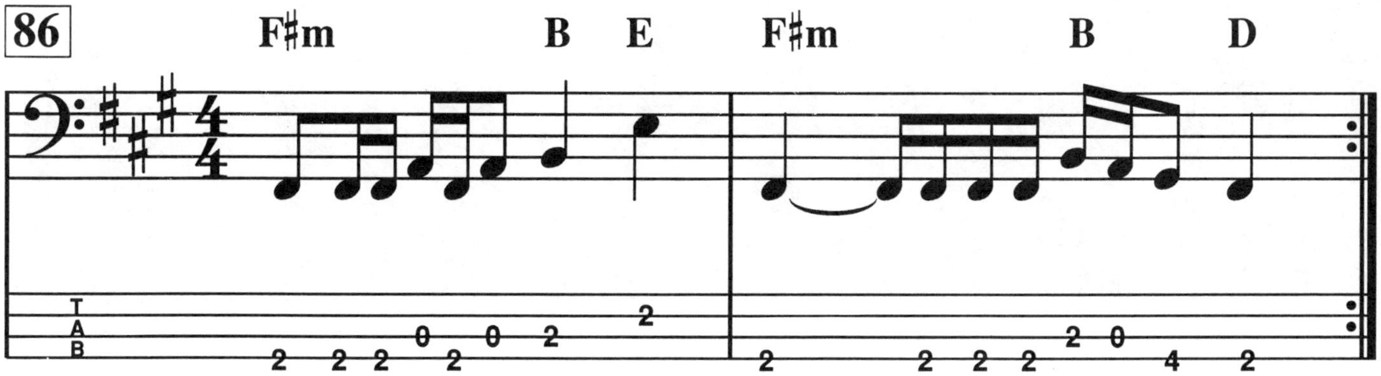

87

Play this lick fast.

88

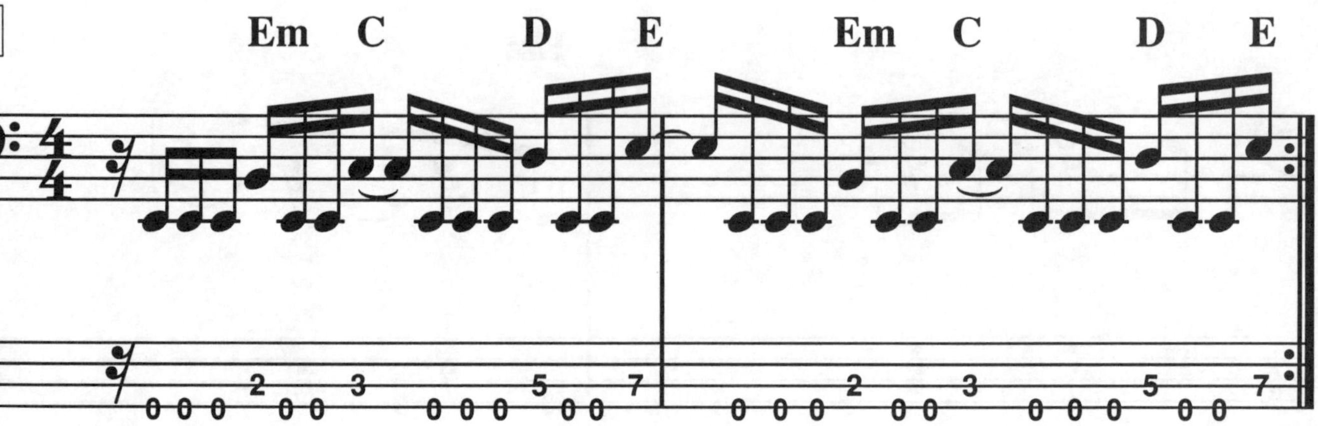

Mr. Big

89

Gm

90

Fm Bb C

91

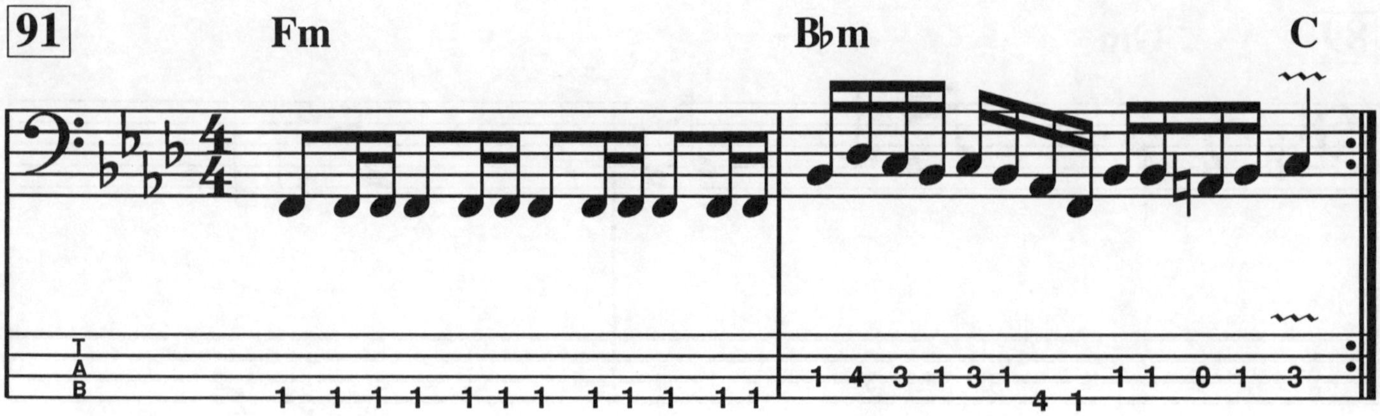

92

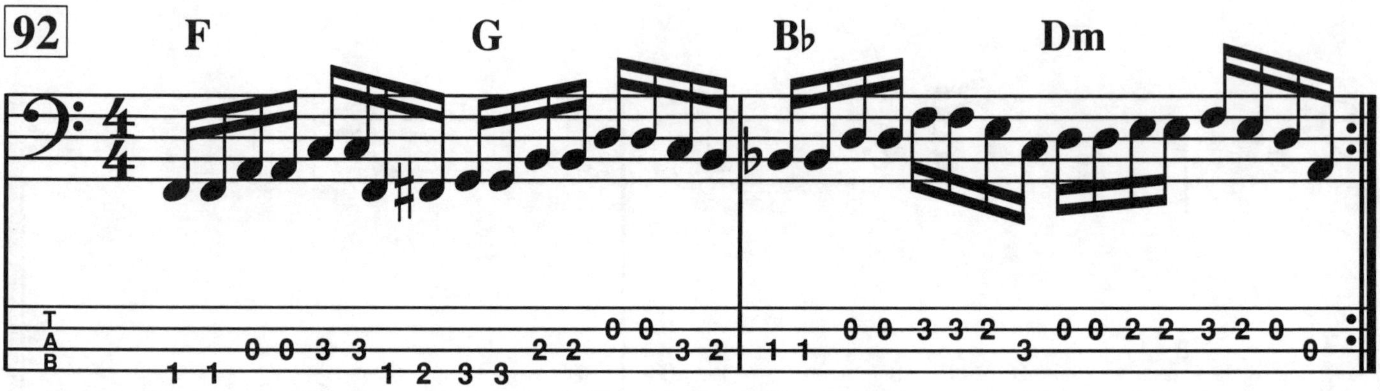

Play the first two bars of this lick several times before ending.

93

94

Brian Wheat (Tesla)

95

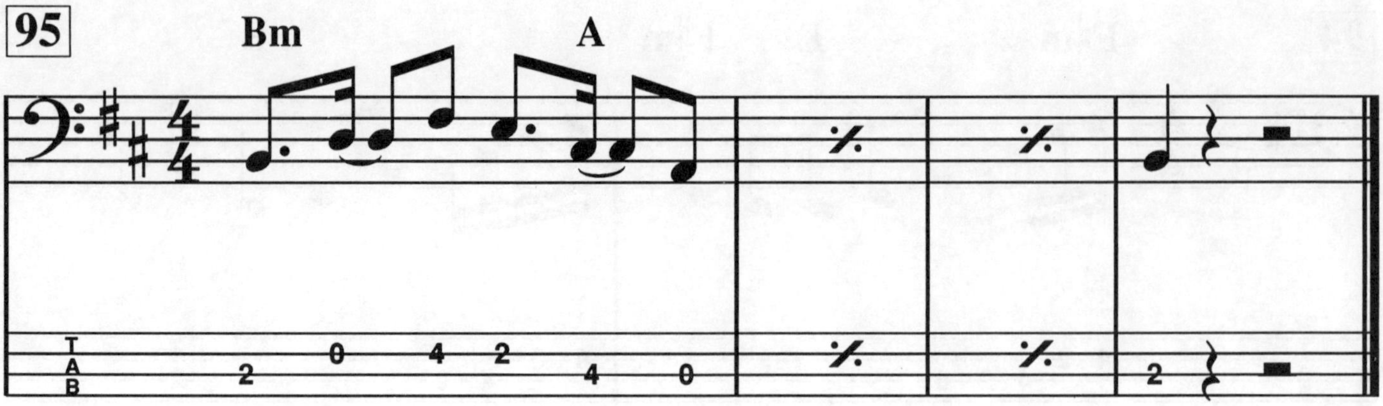

96

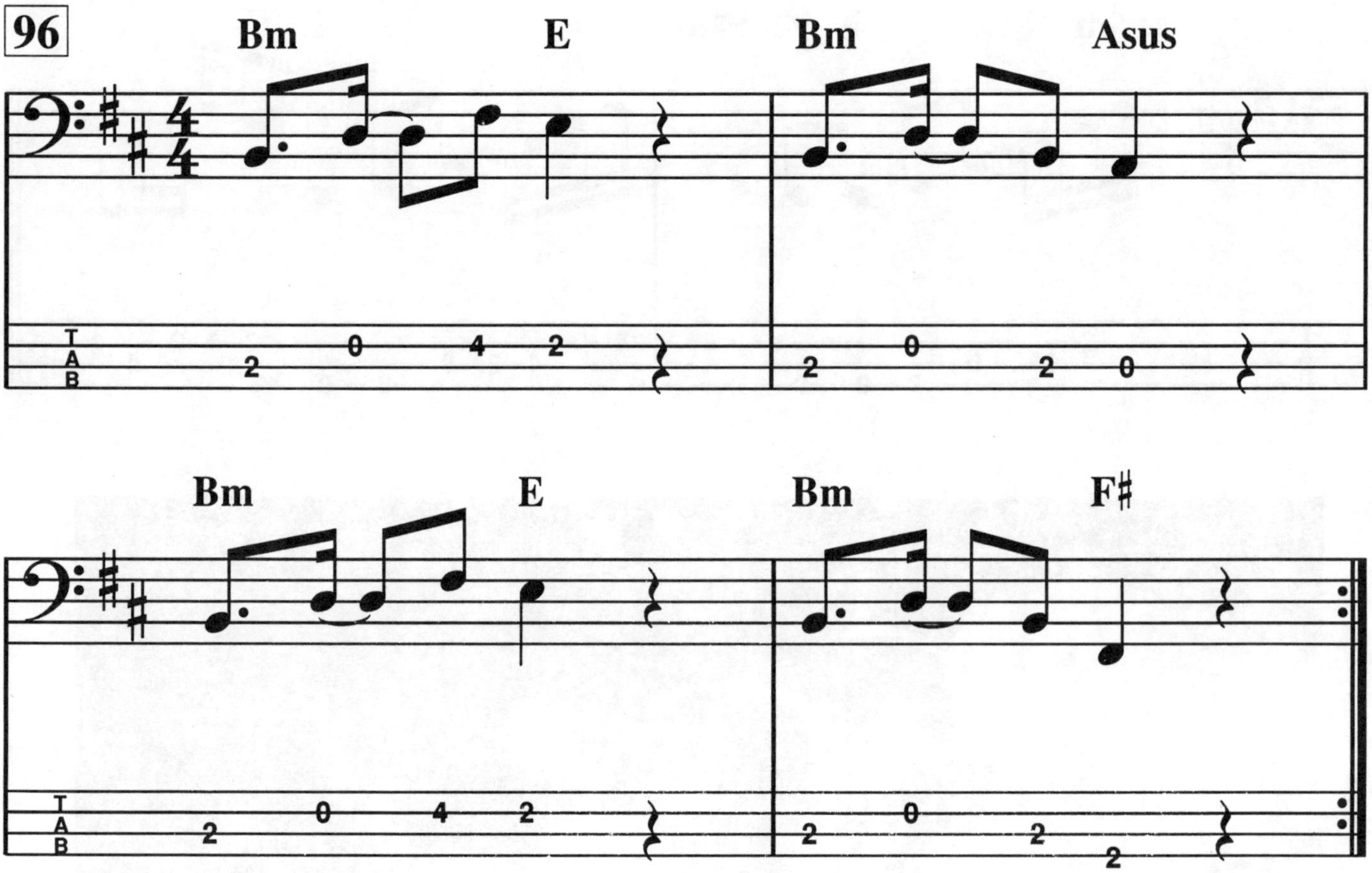

Play Lick 97 with the pick.

97

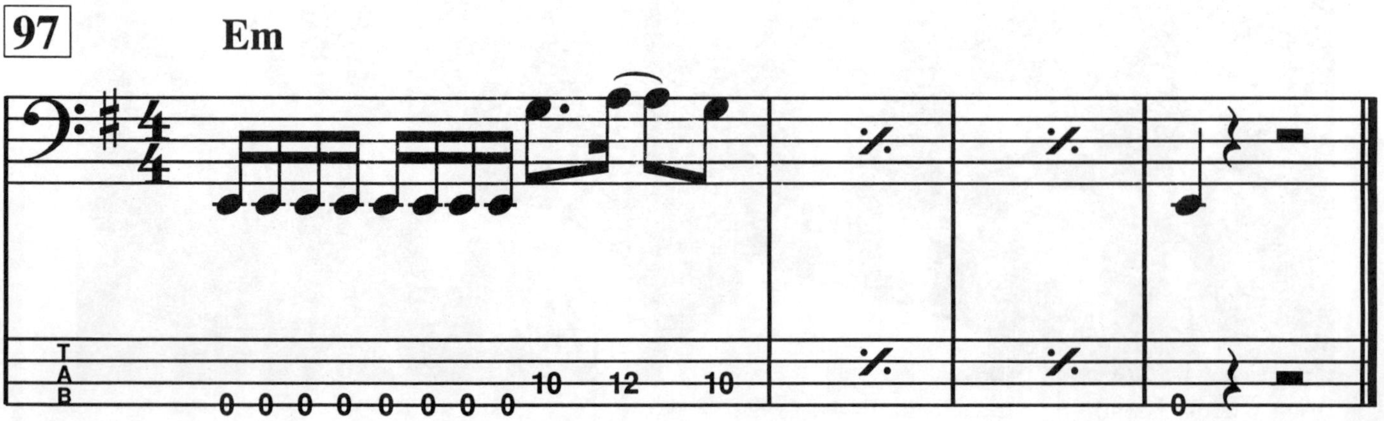

98

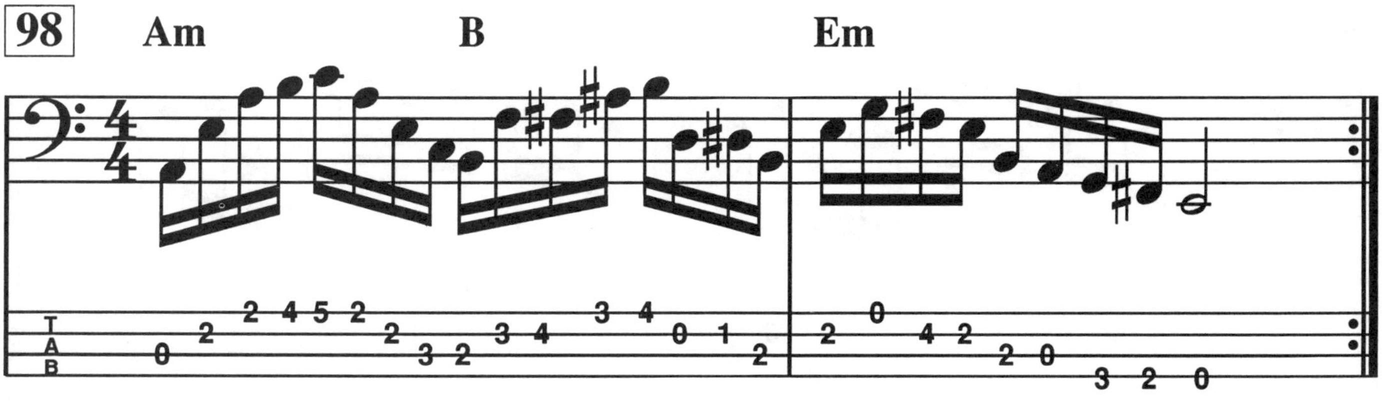

The next two licks are in $\frac{6}{4}$ time.

99

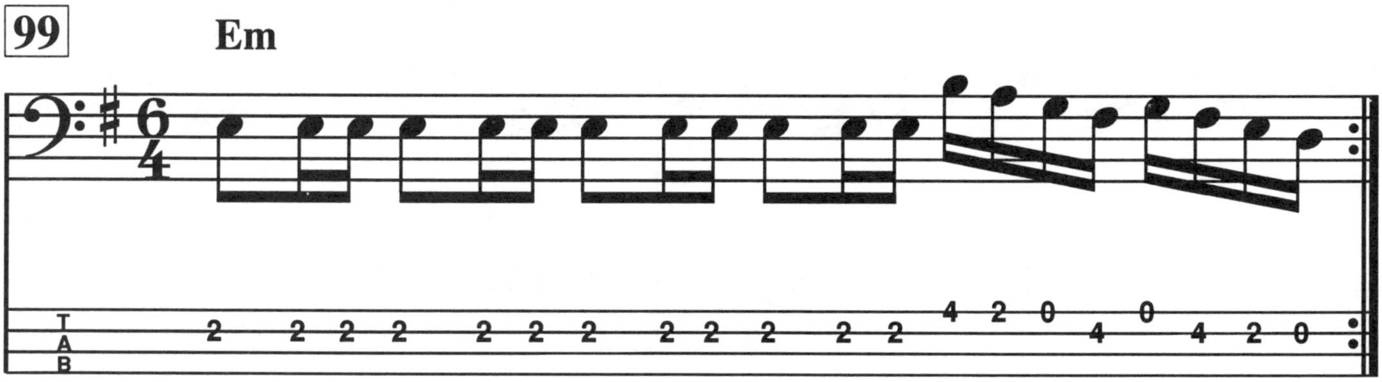

100

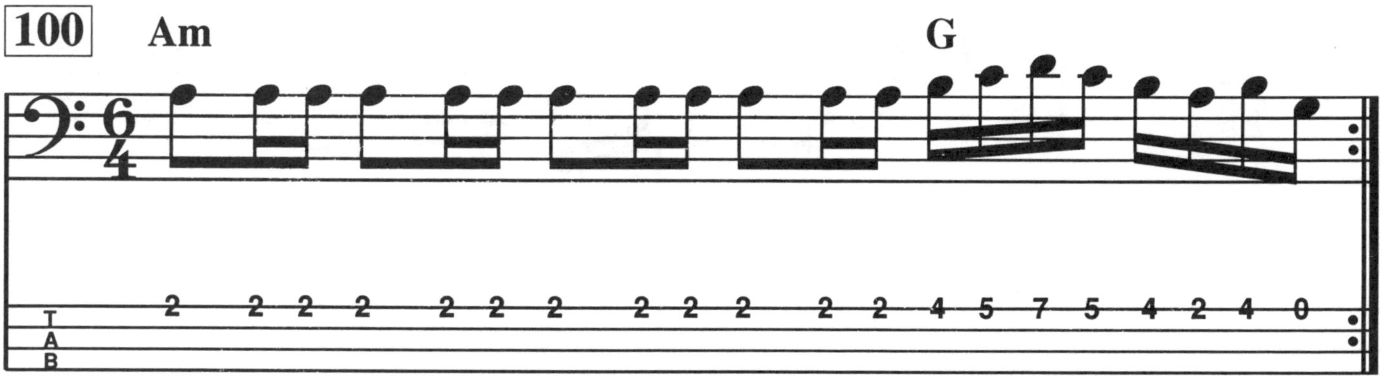

101

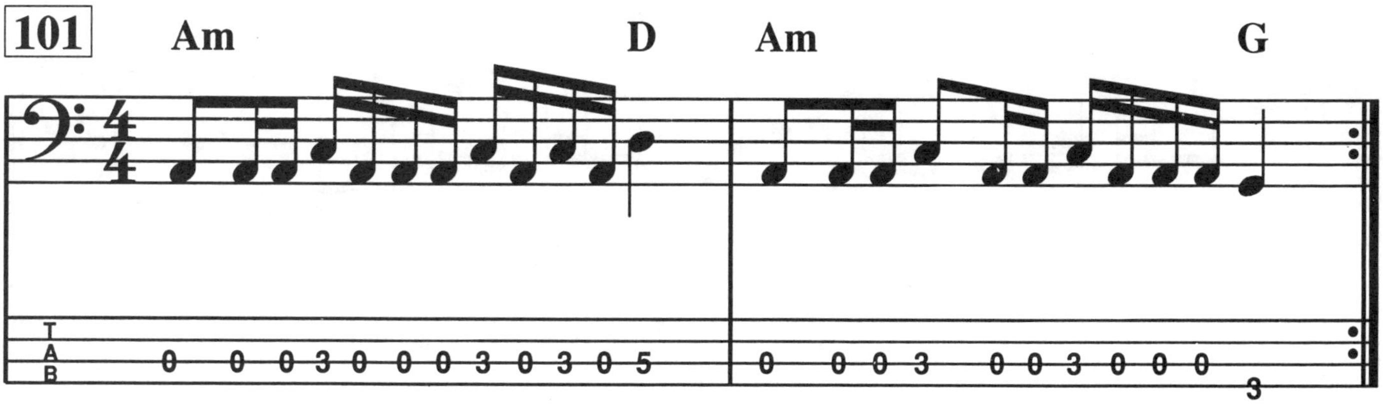

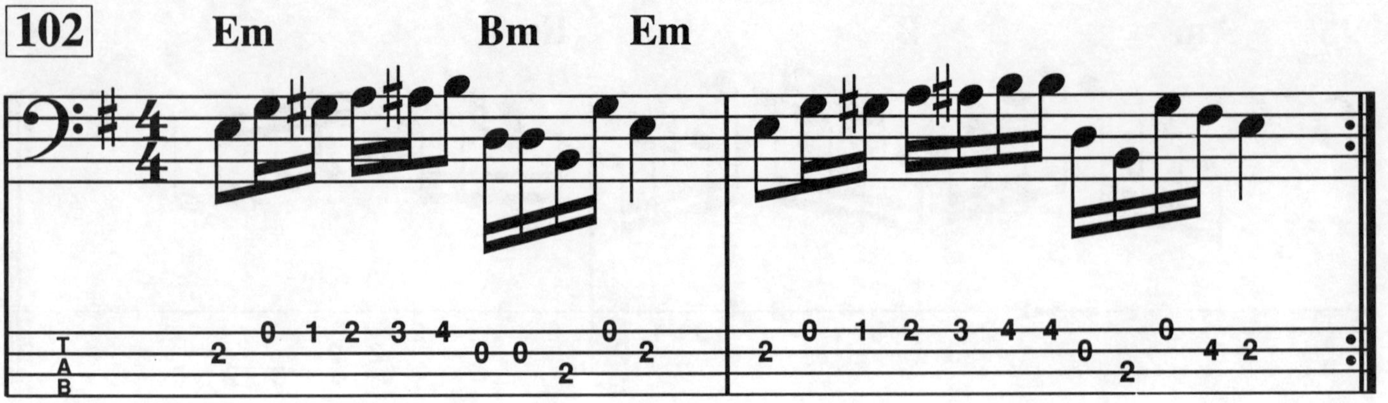
102
Em
Bm
Em
T
A
B

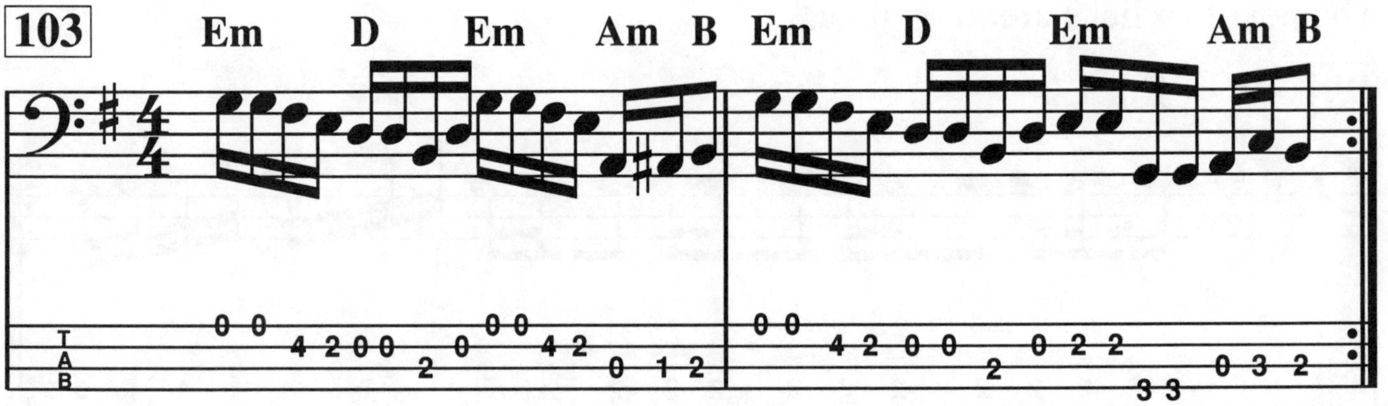
103
Em
D
Em
Am B
Em
D
Em
Am B
T
A
B

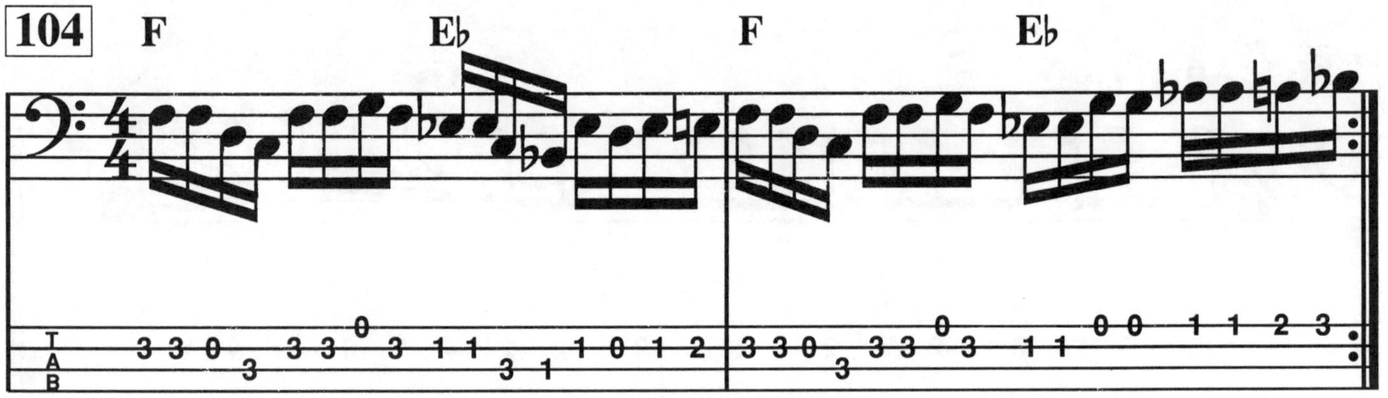
104
F
E♭
F
E♭
T
A
B

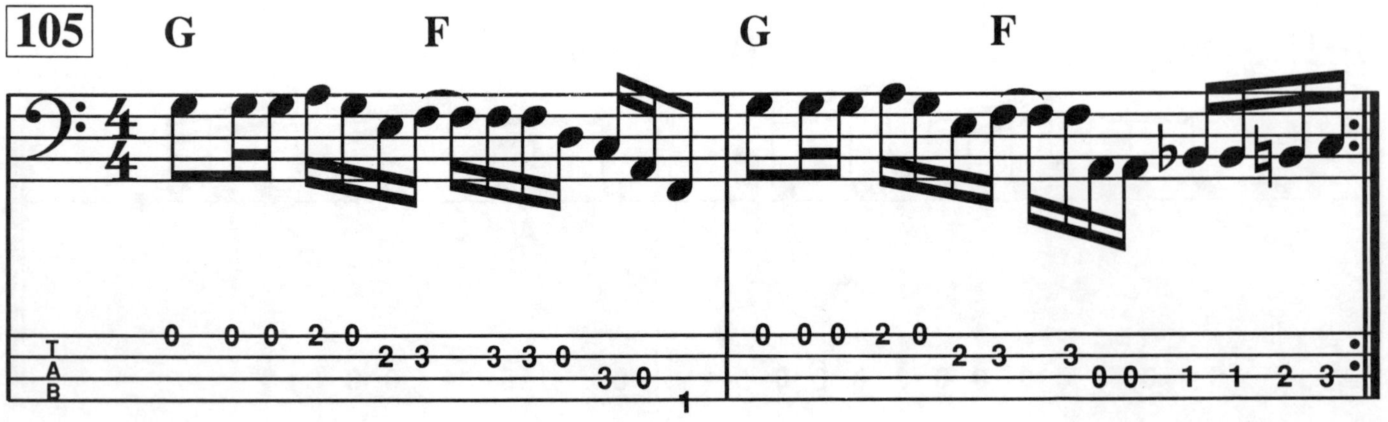
105
G
F
G
F
T
A
B

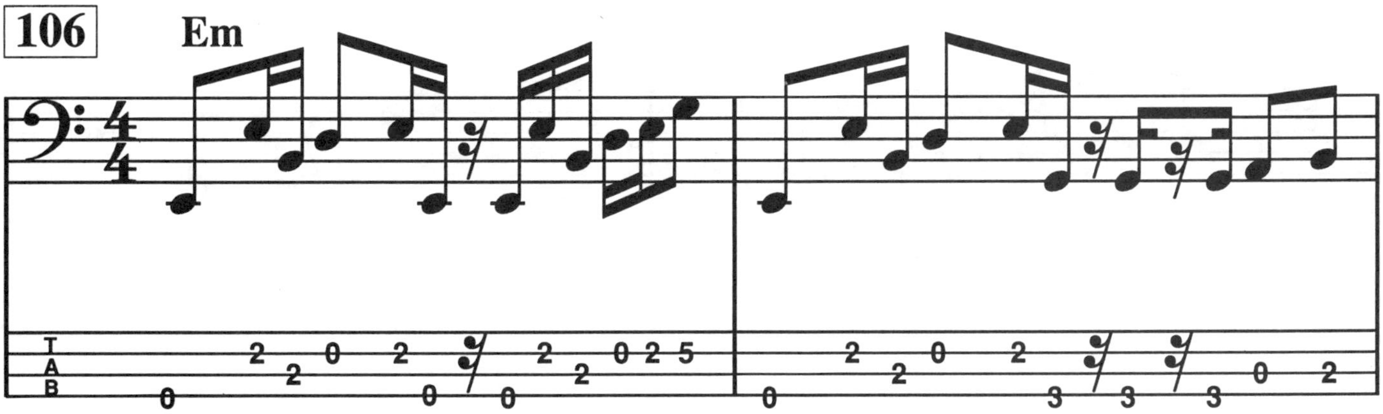

Rudy Sarzo and Adrian Vandenberg

107

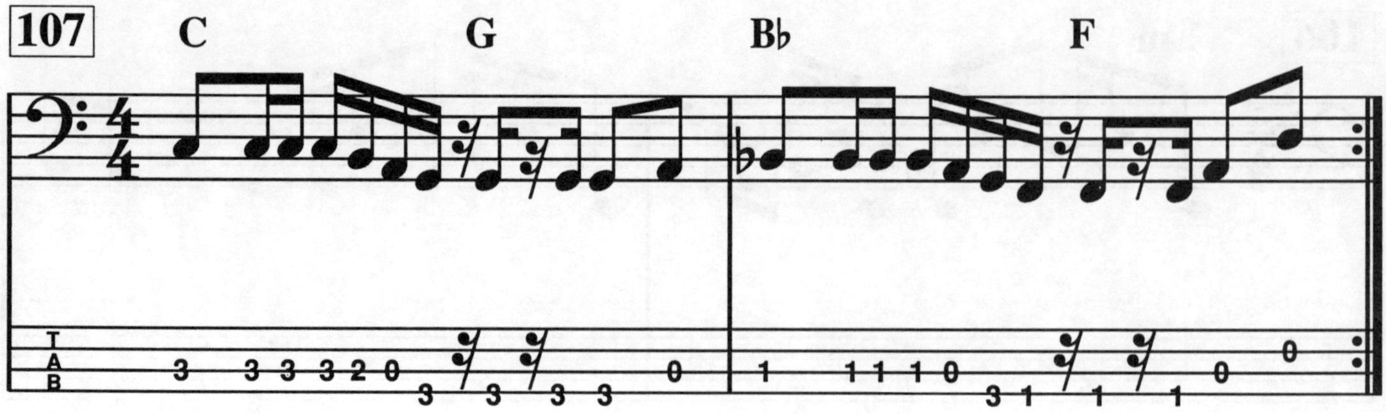

108

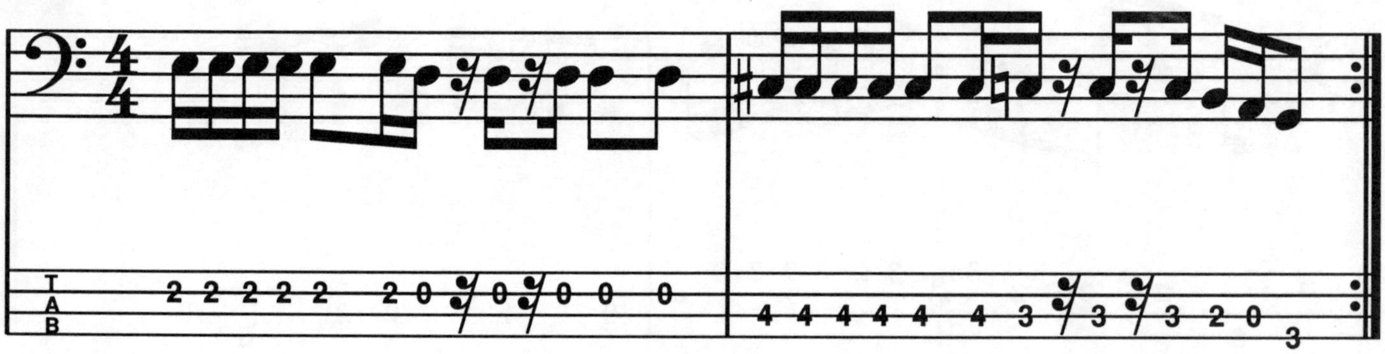

109

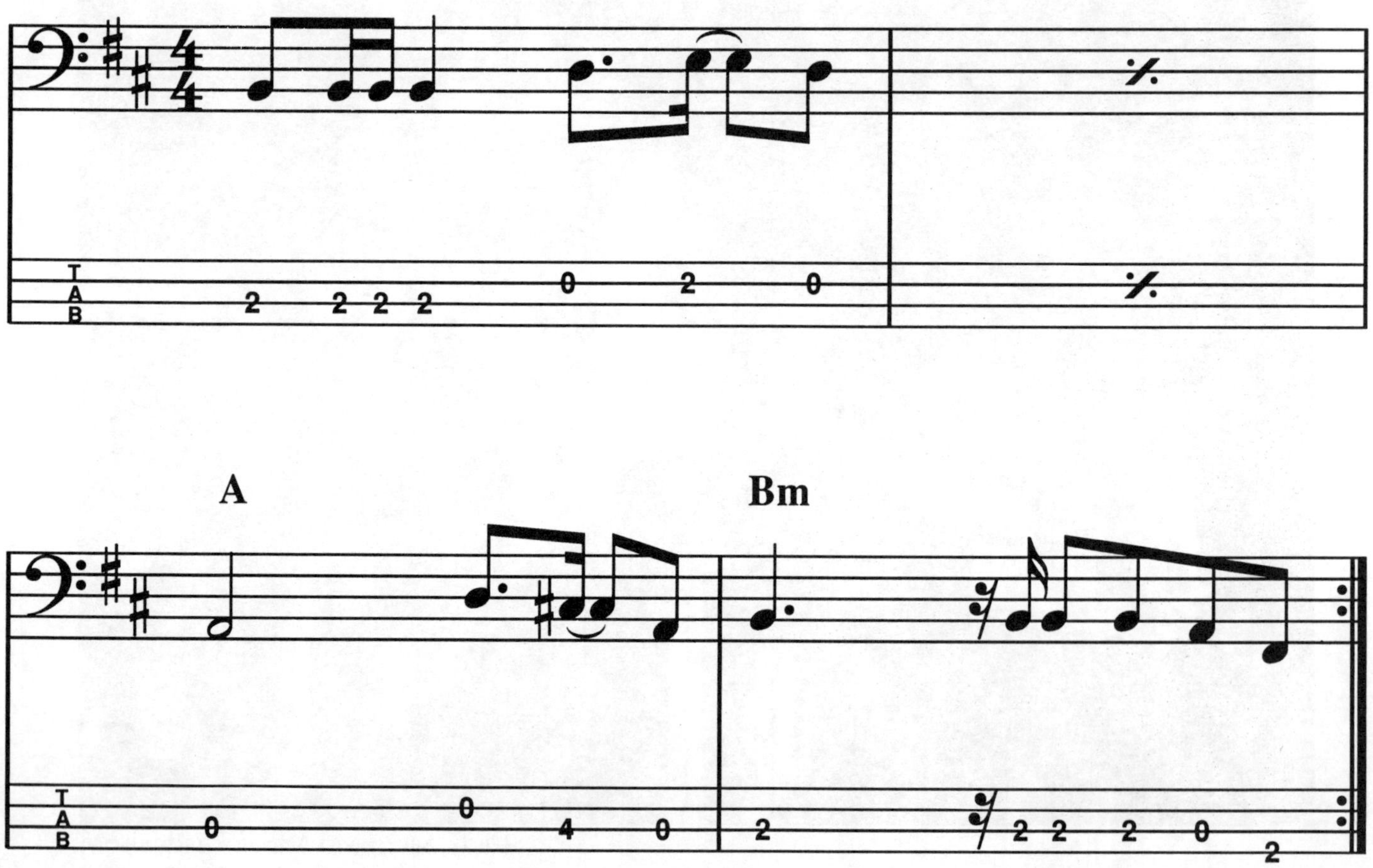

110

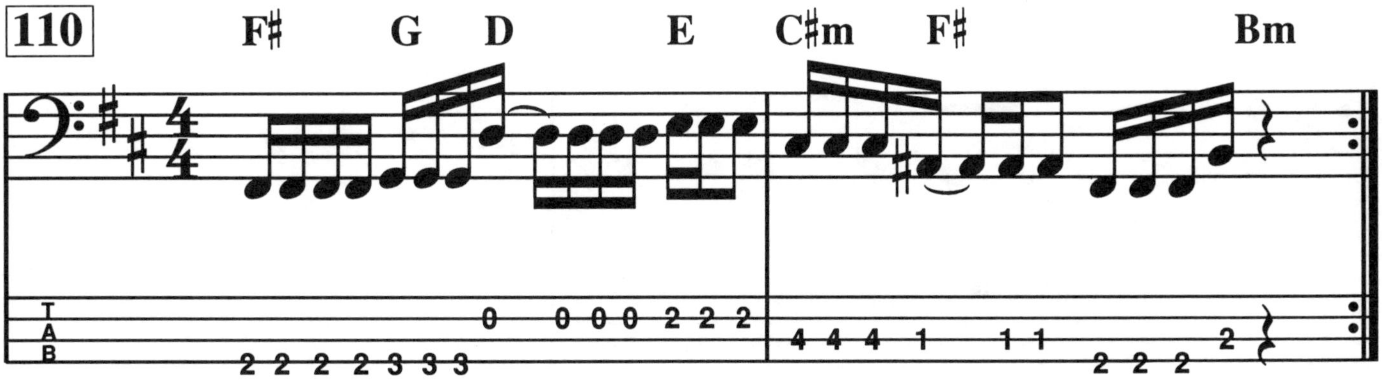

111

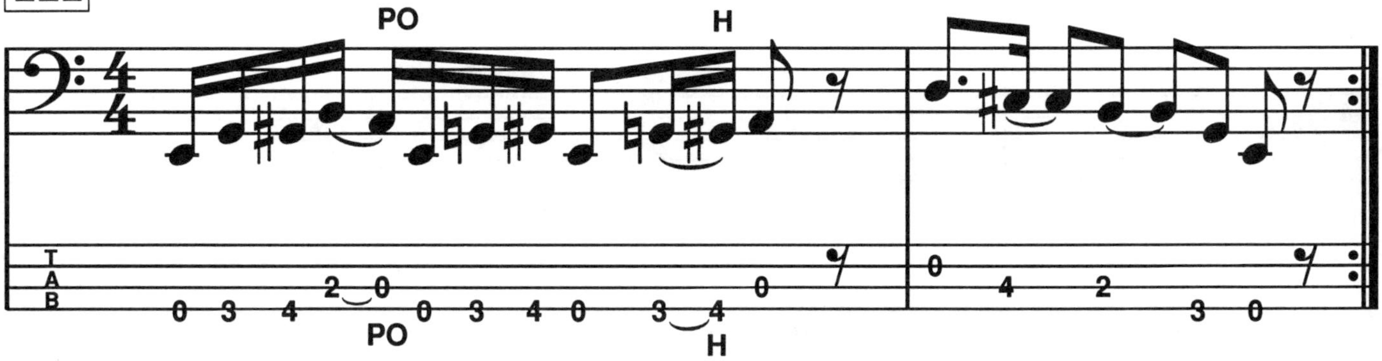

Tune the E string down to the low D note. Let all D notes ring.

112

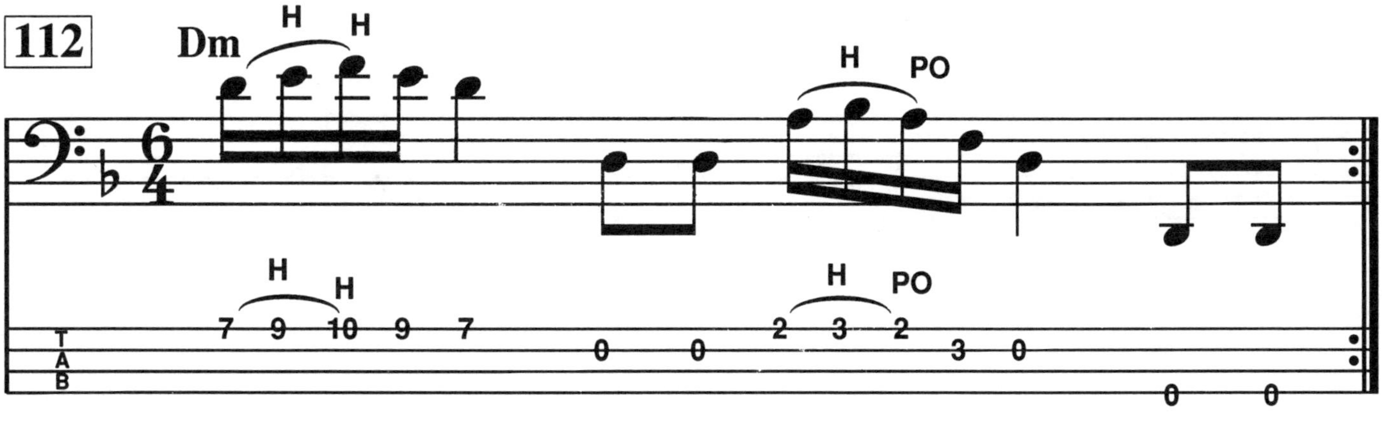

Repeat the first two bars, then play the last bar and go back again to the first two bars.

113

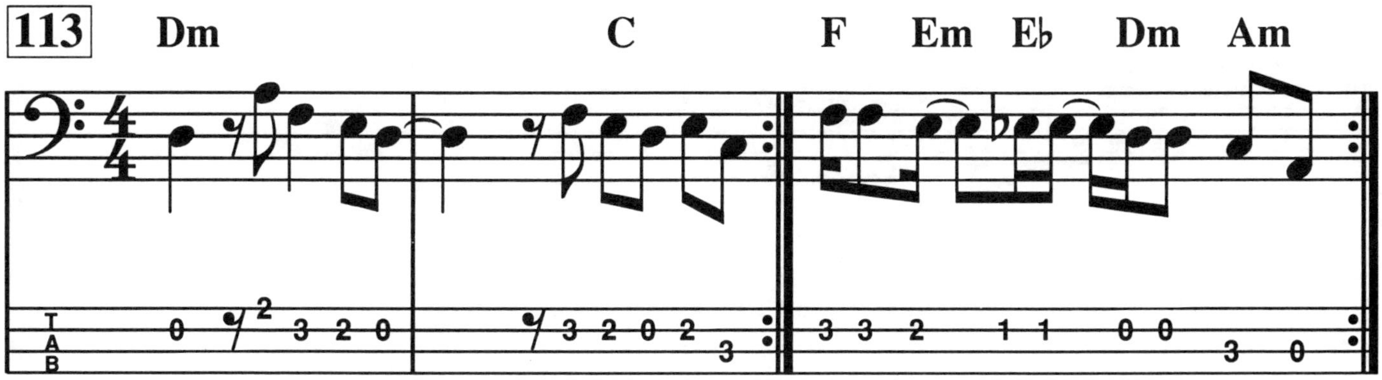

114

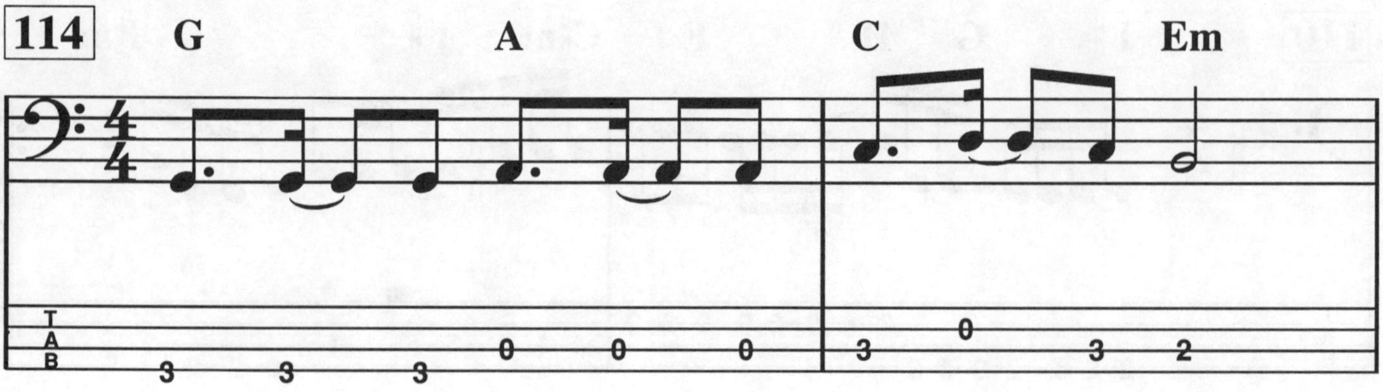

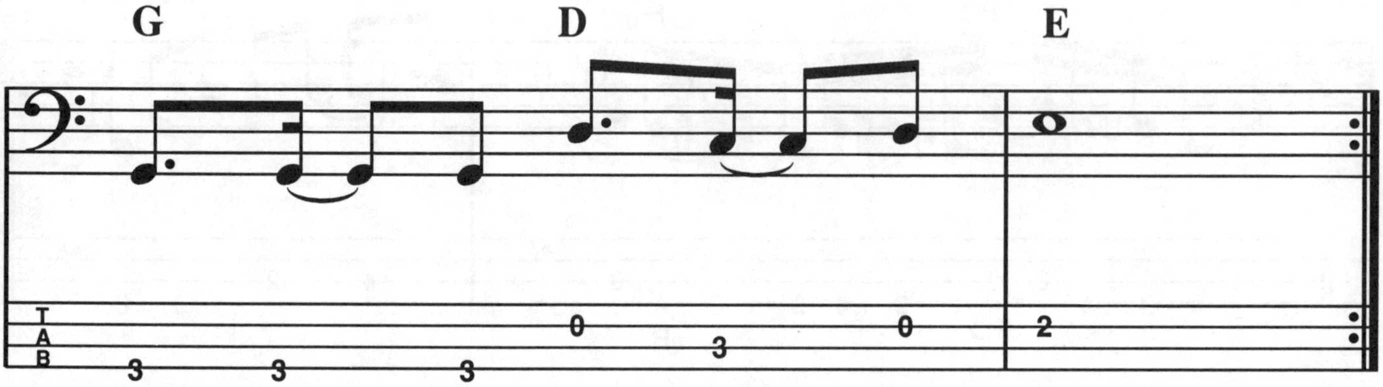

115

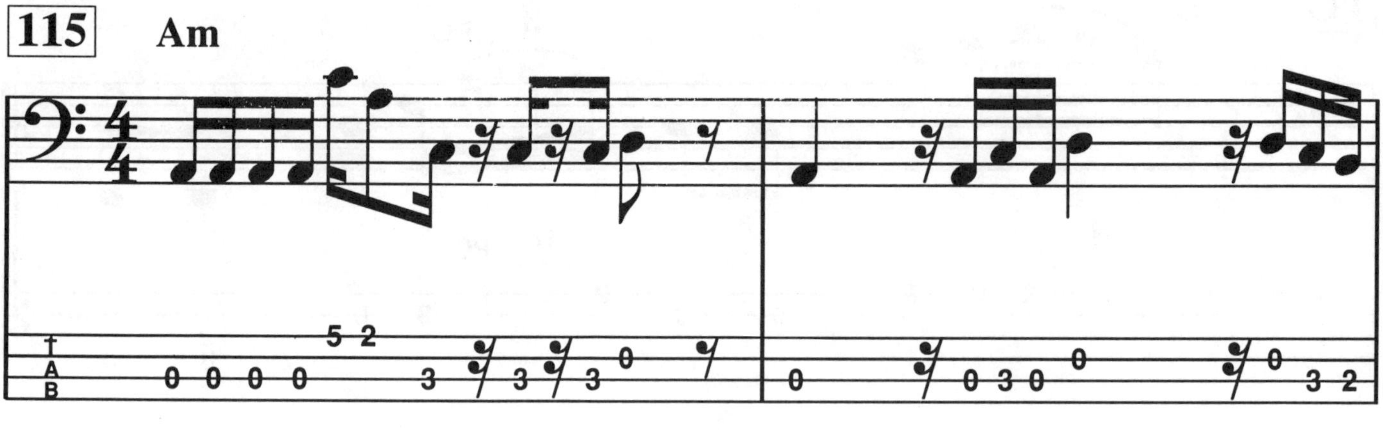

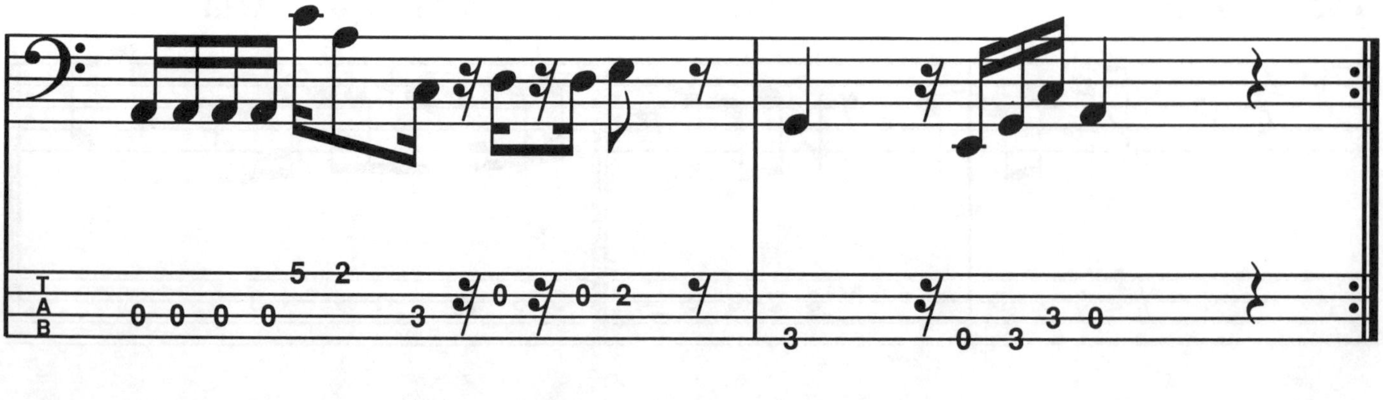

116

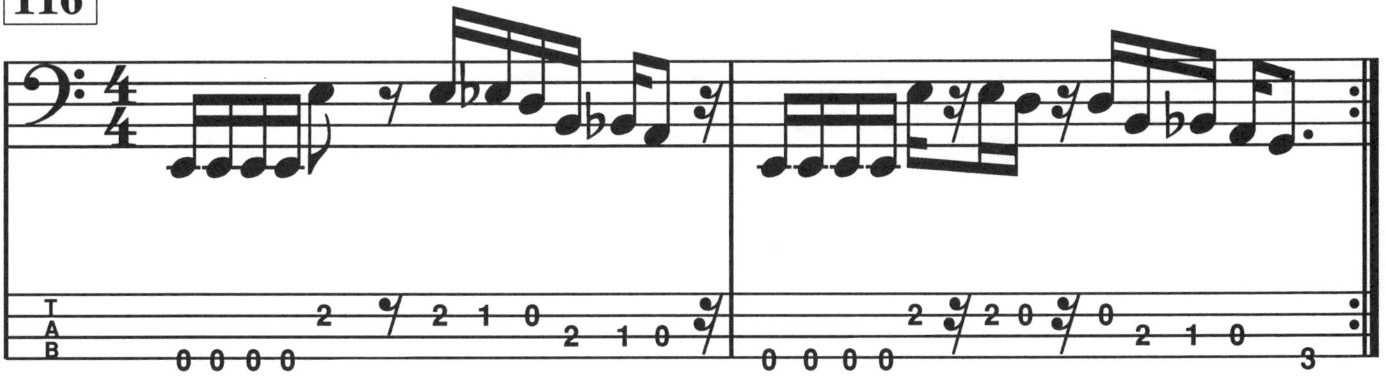

117

118

119

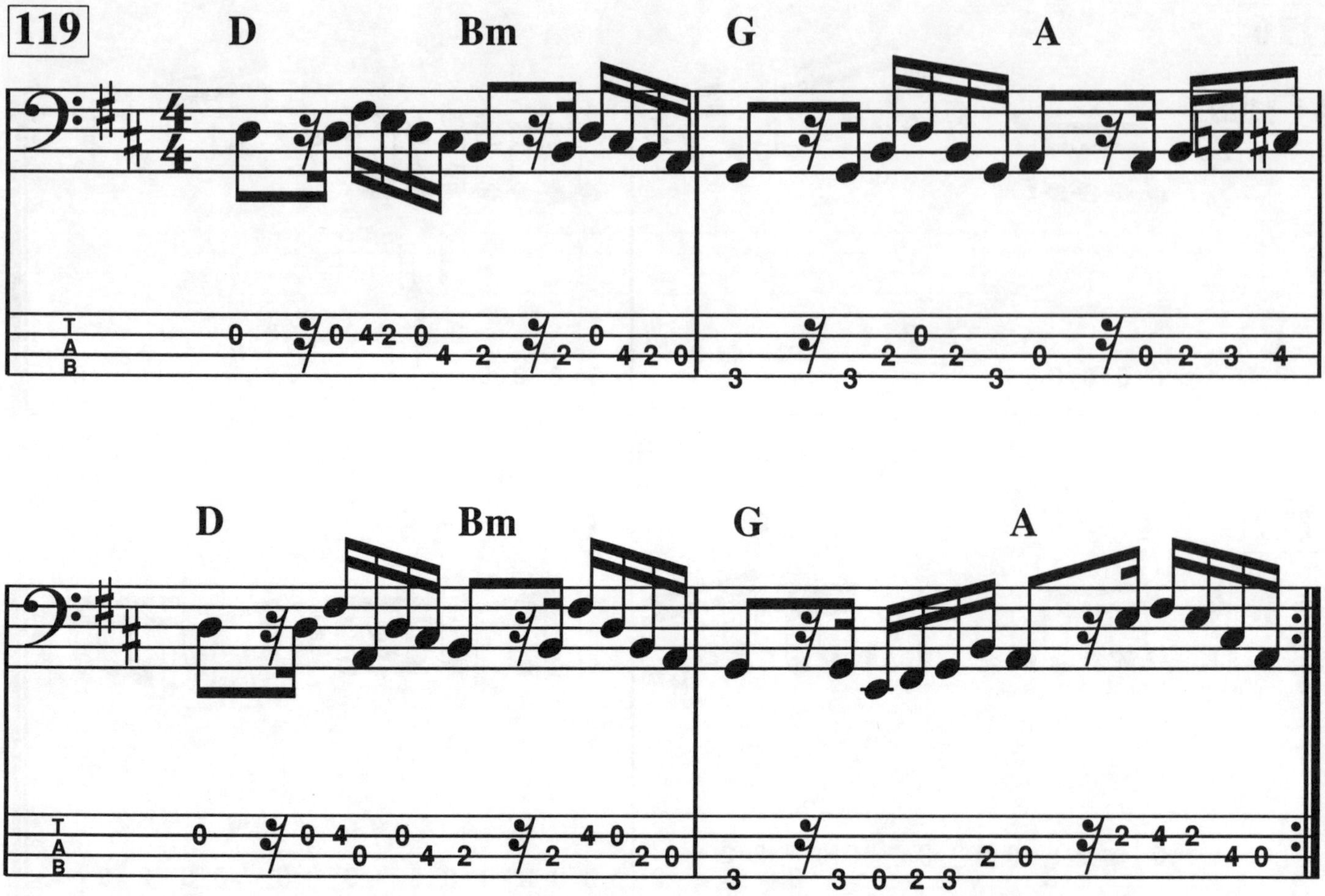

MSG

Listen to the tape to make sure you get the order correct.
After each ending go back to the A section,
i.e. play A A B1, A A B2, A A B3, A A B4.

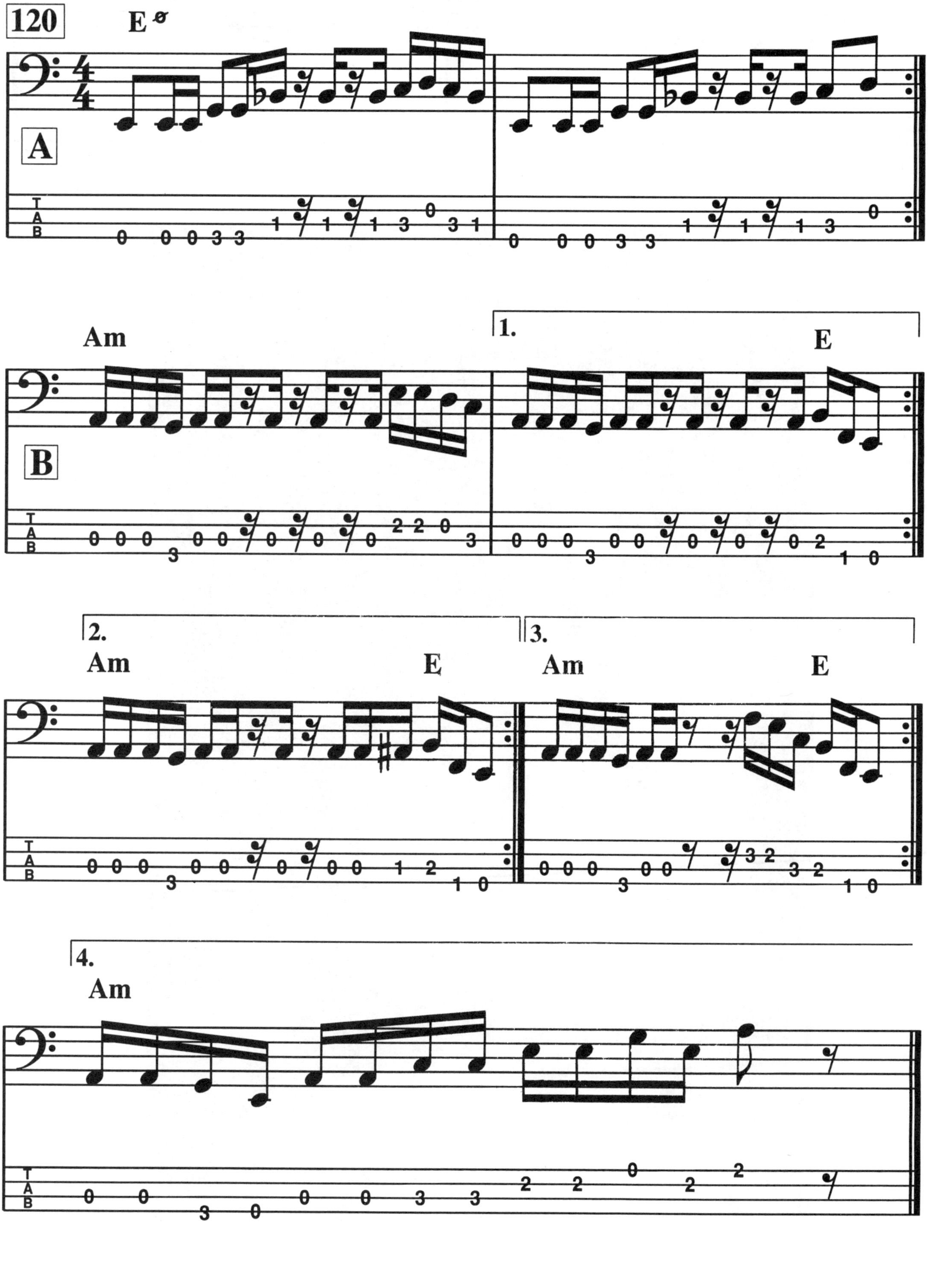

121

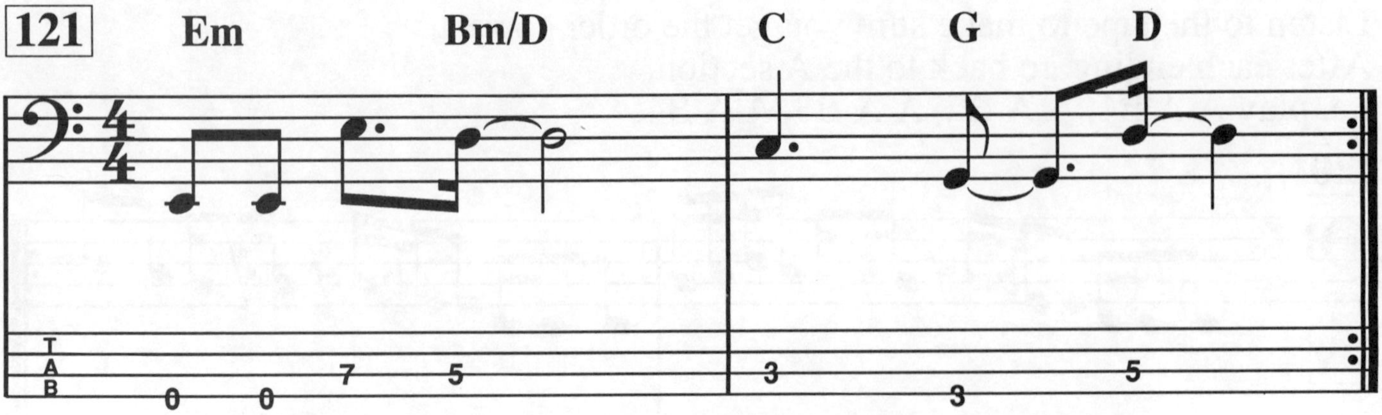

Rick Savage (Def Leppard)

Heavy Metal Slap Licks

This lick is played using the usual finger style.

122

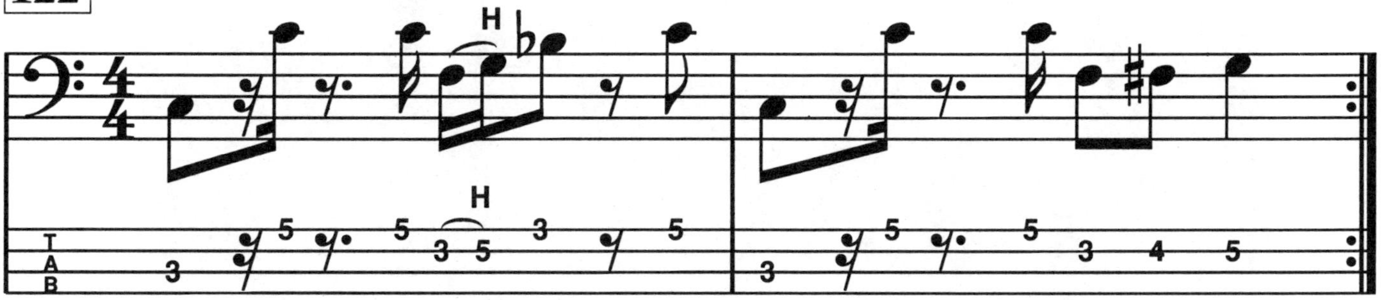

Lick 123 is very similar but arranged for slap playing.

123

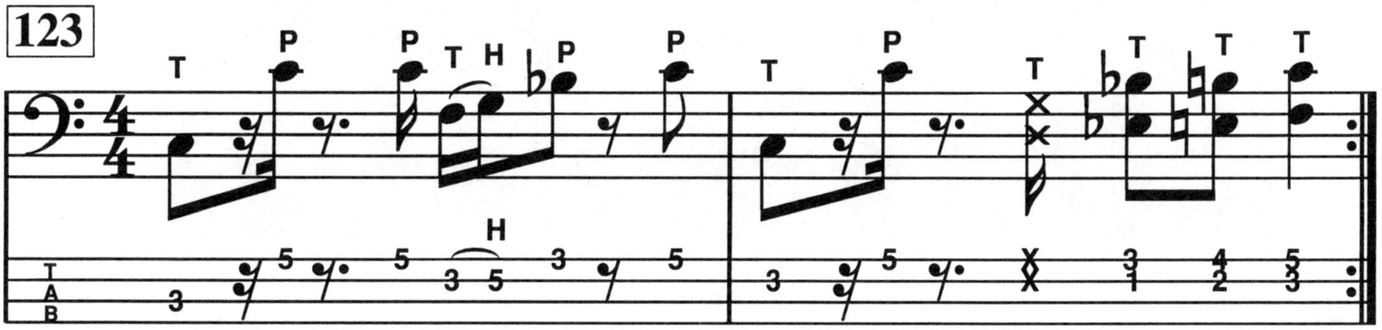

Commence the slide on any of the frets high up on the E string.

124

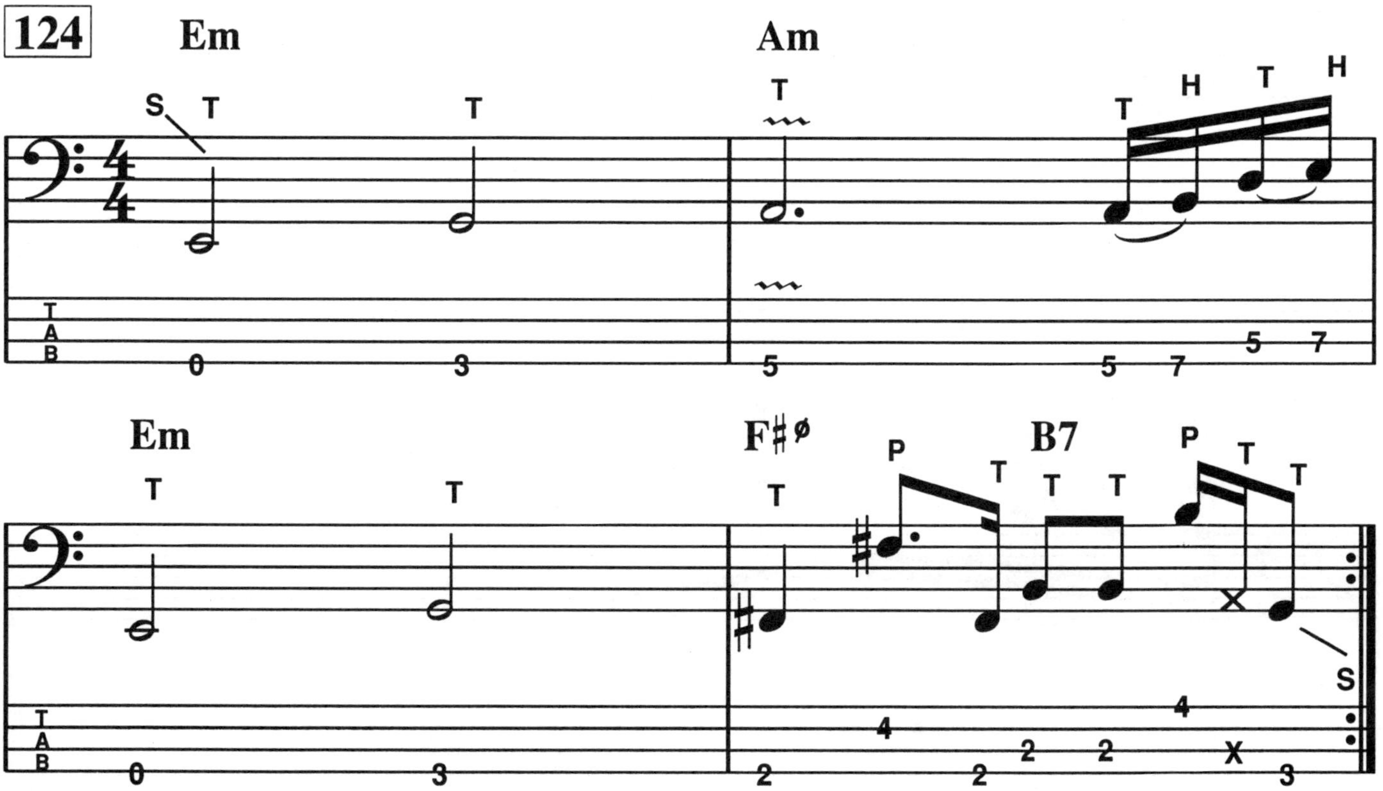

For more information about slapping see Progressive Slap Technique by Stephan Richter.

Heavy Metal Tapping

Stu Hamm

125

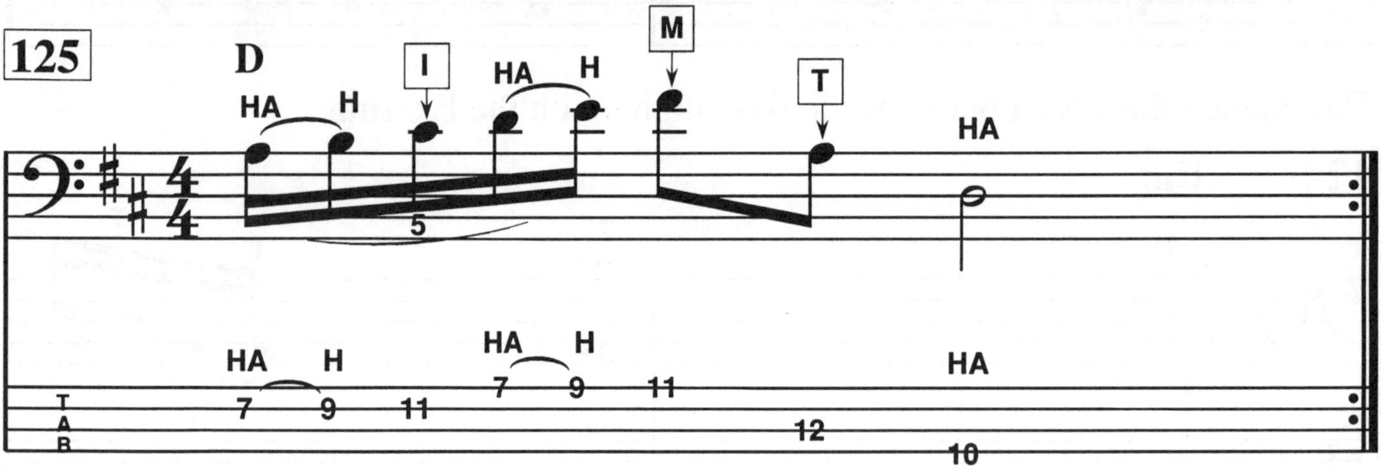

126

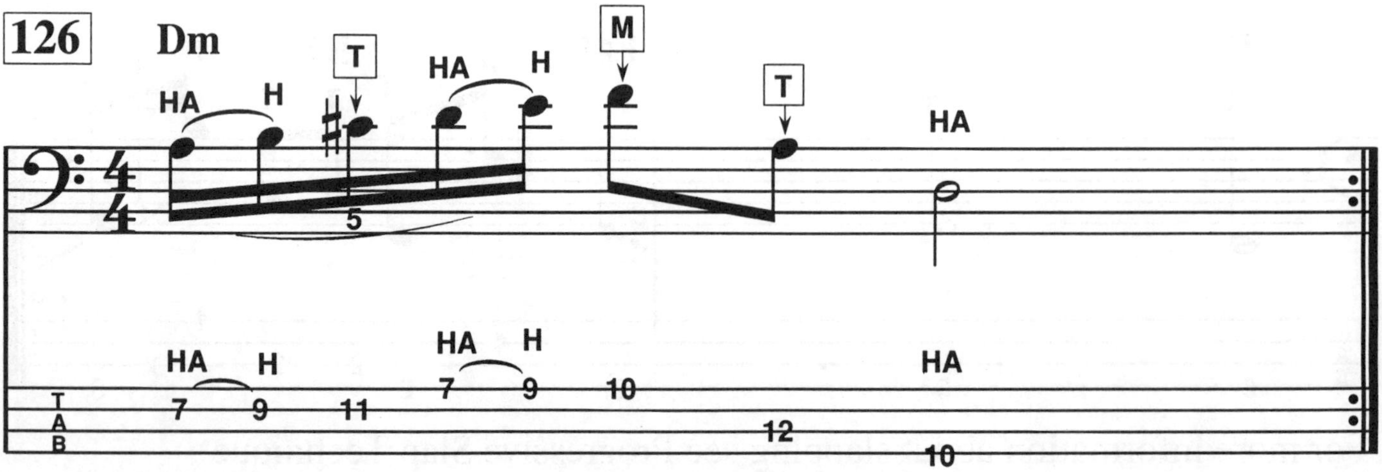

127

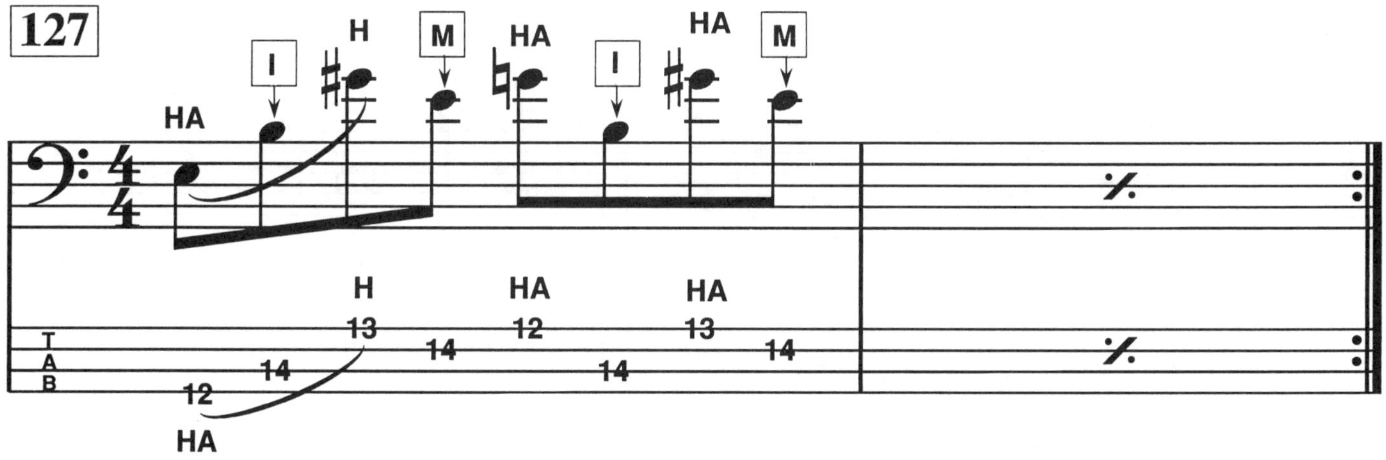

128

129

Am
HA
HA
etc.
Dm
HA
HA
etc.
Am
HA
HA
etc.
Em
I
H
M
HA
etc.
Am
HA
HA
M
I
T
HA
HA
T
A
B

130

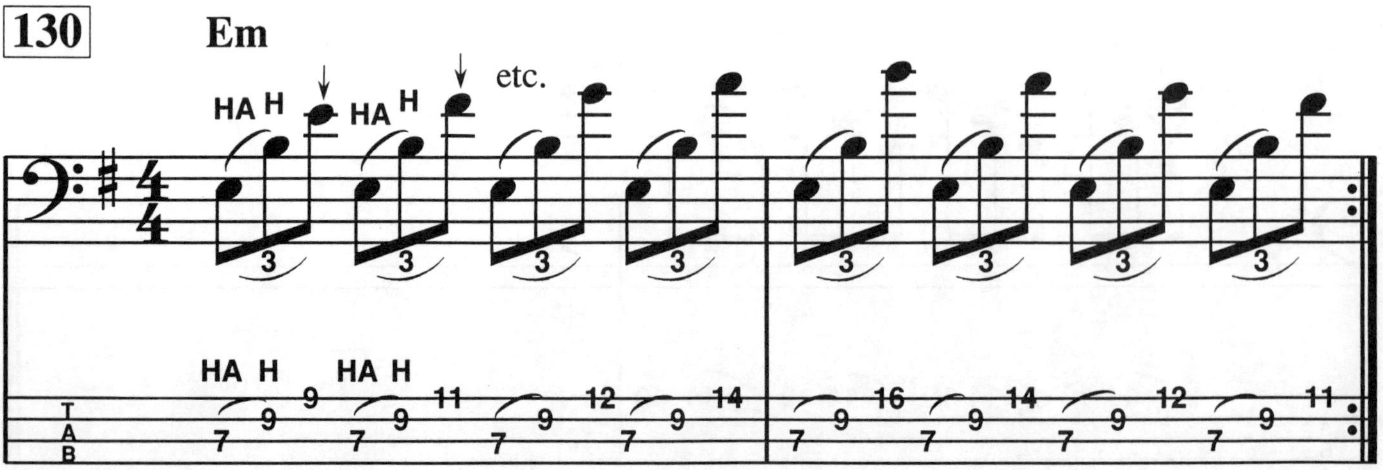
Em
HA H
HA H
etc.
T
A
B

131
Am
HA
H
etc.
HA H HA H
I
M
I
HA
HA

132

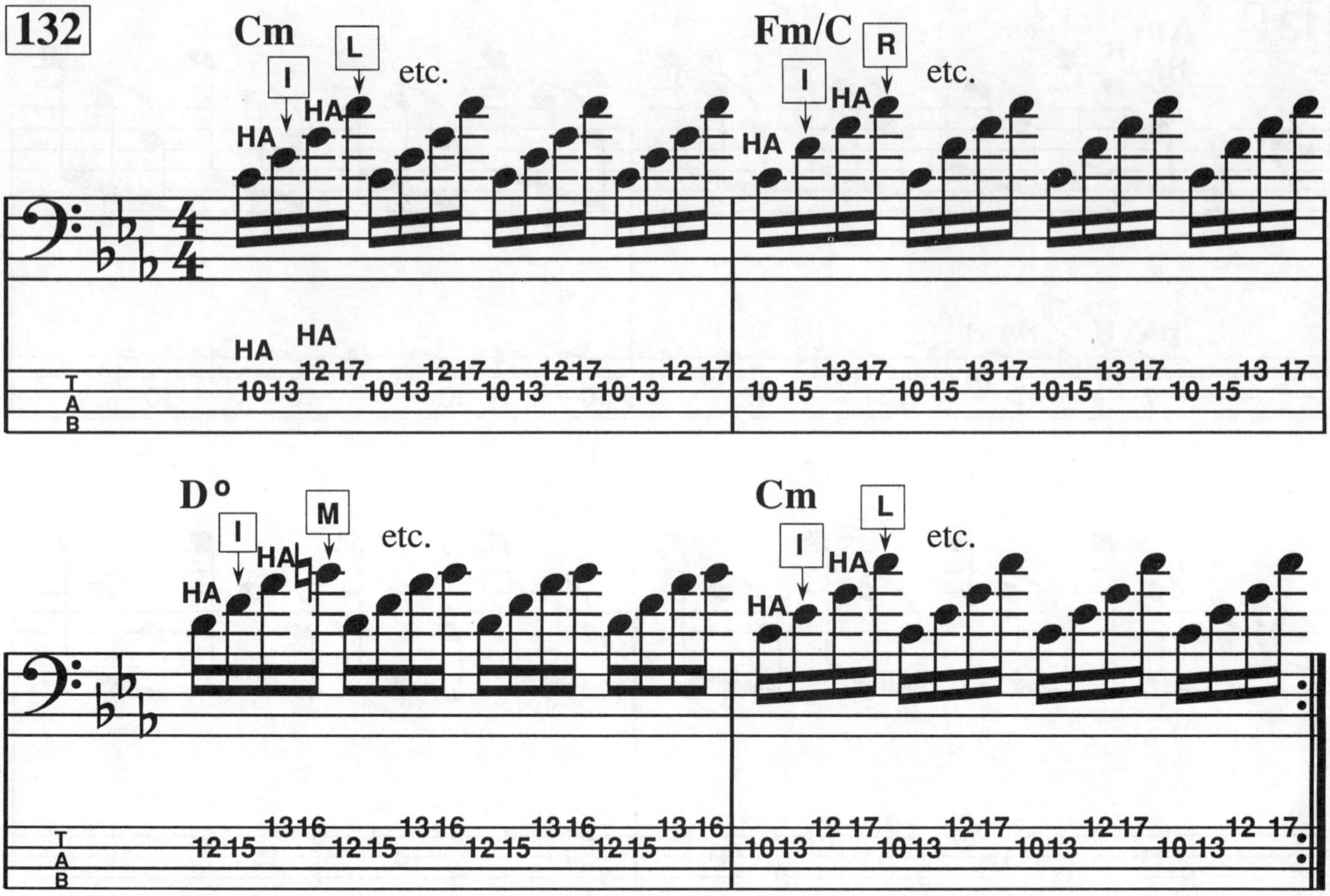
Cm
I
L
HA
HA
etc.
Fm/C
I
R
HA
HA
etc.
HA
HA
10 13 12 17 10 13 12 17 10 13 12 17 10 13 12 17
10 15 13 17 10 15 13 17 10 15 13 17 10 15 13 17
D o
I
M
HA
HA
etc.
Cm
I
L
HA
HA
etc.
12 15 13 16 12 15 13 16 12 15 13 16 12 15 13 16
10 13 12 17 10 13 12 17 10 13 12 17 10 13 12 17

133

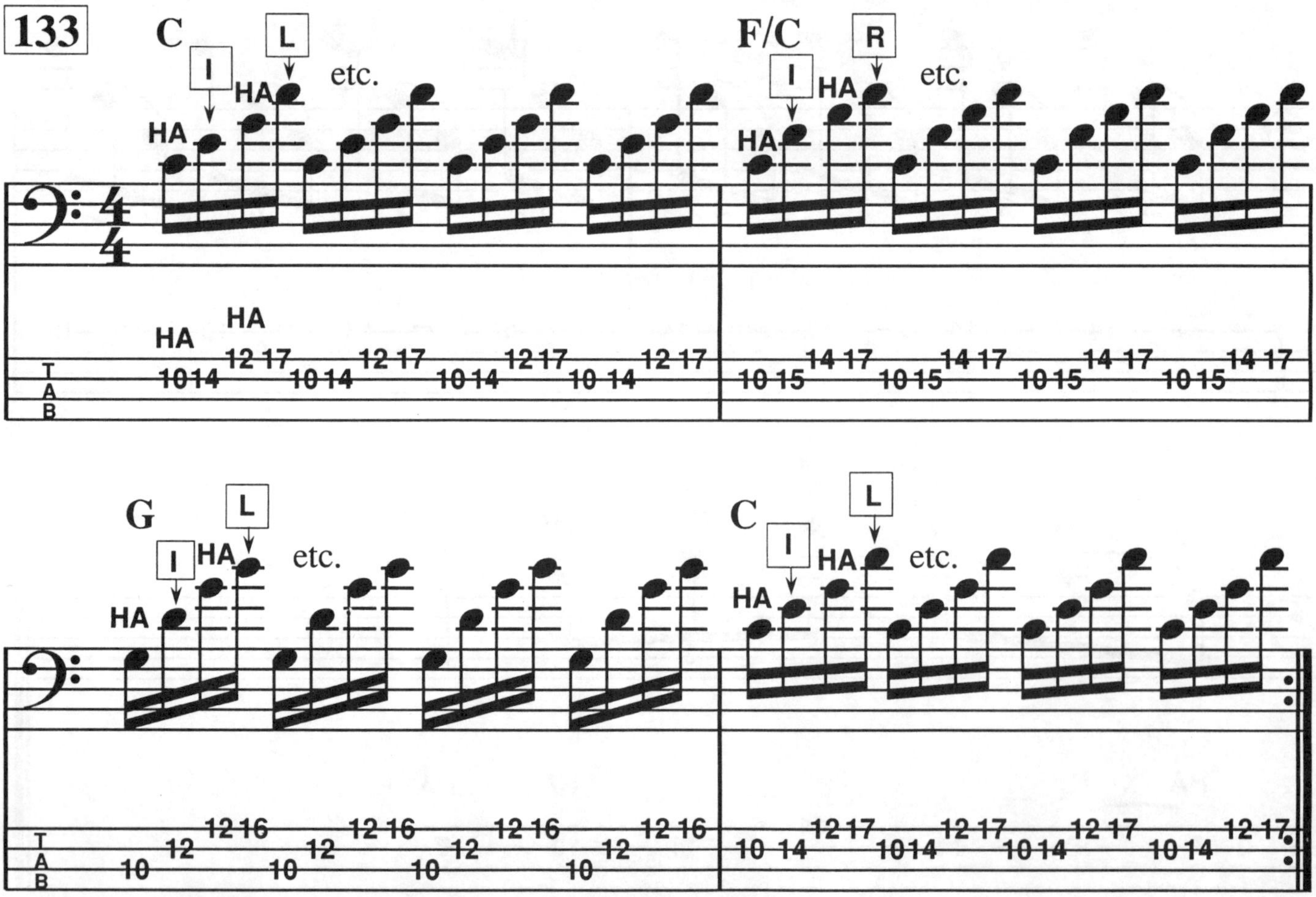
C
I
L
HA
HA
etc.
F/C
I
R
HA
HA
etc.
HA
HA
10 14 12 17 10 14 12 17 10 14 12 17 10 14 12 17
10 15 14 17 10 15 14 17 10 15 14 17 10 15 14 17
G
I
L
HA
HA
etc.
C
I
L
HA
HA
etc.
10 12 12 16 10 12 12 16 10 12 12 16 10 12 12 16
10 14 12 17 10 14 12 17 10 14 12 17 10 14 12 17

134

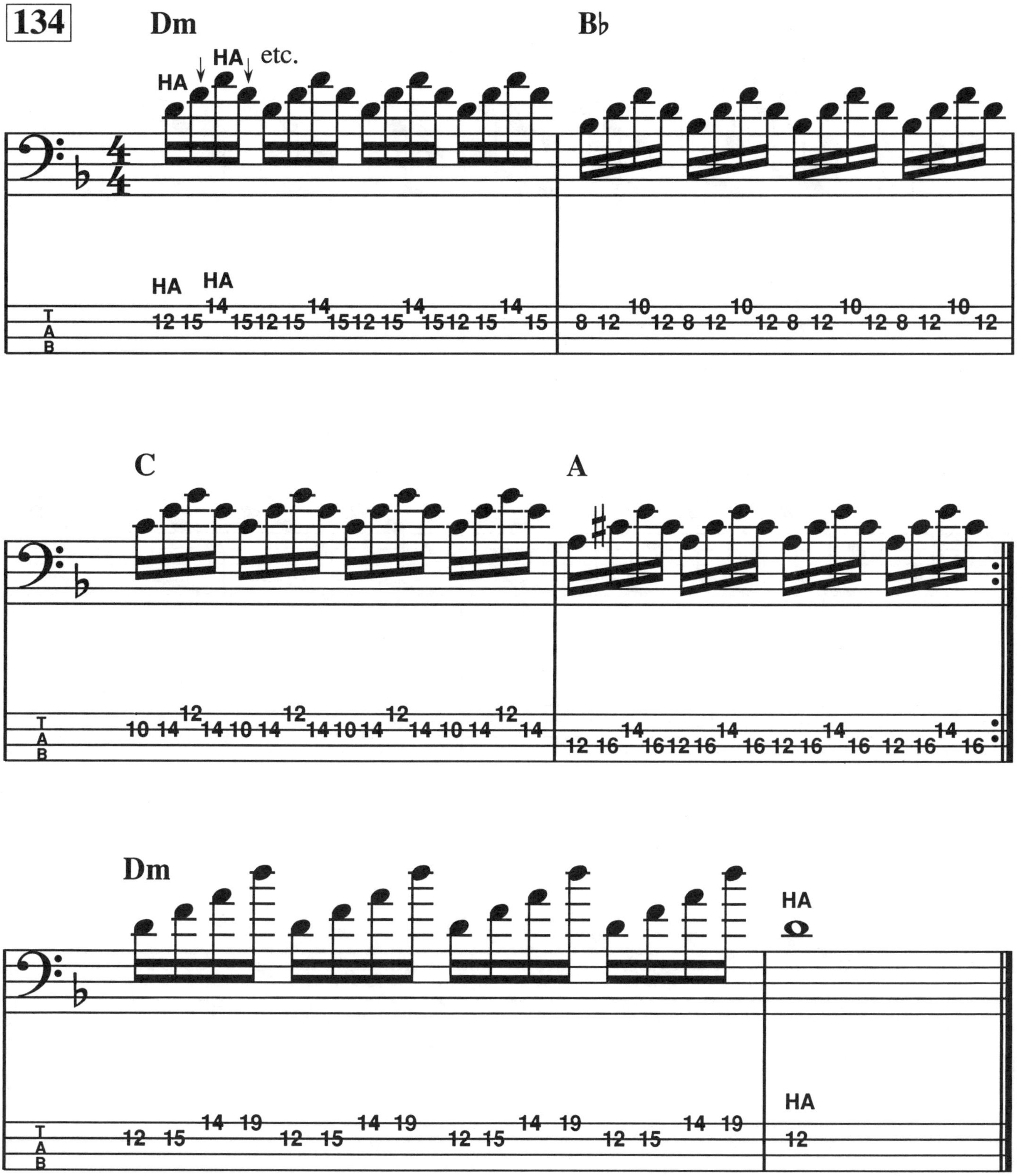
Dm
HA
HA
etc.
B♭
C
A
Dm
HA
HA
12 15 14 15 12 15 14 15 12 15 14 15 12 15 14 15
8 12 10 12 8 12 10 12 8 12 10 12 8 12 10 12
10 14 12 14 10 14 12 14 10 14 12 14 10 14 12 14
12 16 14 16 12 16 14 16 12 16 14 16 12 16 14 16
12 15 14 19 12 15 14 19 12 15 14 19 12 15 14 19
12

For more information about Tapping Technique see Progressive Tapping Technique by Stephan Richter.